MOVIES as MASS COMMUNICATION

DATE DUE

The SAGE CommText Series

Series Editor:
EVERETTE E. DENNIS
Gannett Center for Media Studies, Columbia University

Founding Editor: F. GERALD KLINE, *late of the School of
Journalism and Mass Communication, University of Minnesota*

Founding Associate Editor: SUSAN H. EVANS, *Annenberg School
of Communications, University of Southern California*

The **SAGE CommText** series brings the substance of mass communication scholarship to student audiences by blending syntheses of current research with applied ideas in concise, moderately priced volumes. Designed for use both as supplementary readings and as "modules" with which the teacher can "create" a new text, the **SAGE CommTexts** give students a conceptual map of the field of communication and media research. Some books examine topical areas and issues; others discuss the implications of particular media; still others treat methods and tools used by communication scholars. Written by leading researchers with the student in mind, the **SAGE CommTexts** provide teachers in communication and journalism with solid supplementary materials.

Available in this series:

1. TELEVISION IN AMERICA
   George Comstock
2. COMMUNICATION HISTORY
   *John D. Stevens and
   Hazel Dicken Garcia*
3. PRIME-TIME TELEVISION:
   Content and Control
   Muriel G. Cantor
4. MOVIES AS MASS COMMUNICATION,
   Second Edition
   *Garth Jowett and
   James M. Linton*
5. CONTENT ANALYSIS:
   An Introduction to Its Methodology
   Klaus Krippendorff
6. INTERPERSONAL COMMUNICATION:
   The Social Exchange Approach
   Michael E. Roloff
7. THE CARTOON:
   Communication to the Quick
   Randall P. Harrison
8. ADVERTISING AND SOCIAL CHANGE
   Ronald Berman
9. COMPARATIVE COMMUNICATION
   RESEARCH
   Alex S. Edelstein
10. MEDIA ANALYSIS TECHNIQUES
    Arthur Asa Berger
11. SHAPING THE FIRST AMENDMENT:
    The Development of Free Expression
    John D. Stevens

12. THE SOAP OPERA
    *Muriel G. Cantor and
    Suzanne Pingree*
13. THE DISSIDENT PRESS: Alternative
    Journalism in American History
    Lauren Kessler
14. TELEVISION AND CHILDREN: A Special
    Medium for a Special Audience
    Aimée Dorr
15. PRECISION JOURNALISM:
    A Practical Guide
    *David Pearce Demers
    and Suzanne Nichols*
16. PUBLIC RELATIONS:
    What Research Tells Us
    John V. Pavlik
17. NEW ELECTRONIC PATHWAYS:
    Videotex, Teletext, and
    Online Databases
    Jerome Aumente
18. THE TELEVISION NEWS INTERVIEW
    Akiba A. Cohen
19. UNDERSTANDING VIDEO:
    Applications, Impact, and Theory
    Jarice Hanson
20. EXAMINING NEWSPAPERS:
    What Research Reveals About
    America's Newspapers
    Gerald Stone
21. CRITICIZING THE MEDIA:
    Empirical Approaches
    James B. Lemert

additional titles in preparation

Garth Jowett
James M. Linton

MOVIES as
MASS
COMMUNICATION

Second Edition

Volume 4. The Sage COMMTEXT Series

SAGE PUBLICATIONS
The Publishers of Professional Social Science
Newbury Park   London   New Delhi

For Patricia, who provides the enthusiasm, knowledge and encouragement . . .
and Shirley, Aaron and Melissa whose continuing understanding and
support made this project — and all else — possible.

For information address:

SAGE Publications, Inc.
2111 West Hillcrest Drive
Newbury Park, California 91320

SAGE Publications Ltd.
28 Banner Street
London EC1Y 8QE
England

SAGE Publications India Pvt. Ltd.
M-32 Market
Greater Kailash I
New Delhi 110 048 India

Printed in the United States of America

Library of Congress Cataloging-in-Publication Data

Jowett, Garth.
    Movies as mass communication / Garth Jowett, James M. Linton. —
2nd ed.
        p.   cm. — (The Sage commtext series ; v. 4)
    Includes bibliographical references.
    ISBN 0-8039-3328-2. — ISBN 0-8039-3329-0 (pbk.)
    1. Motion picture industry — United States.   2. Mass media — United
States.   I. Linton, James M.   II. Title.   III. Series.
PN1993.5.U6S68   1989
302.23'43 — dc20   89-35235
                                                                       CIP

FIRST PRINTING, SECOND EDITION, 1989

CONTENTS

ACKNOWLEDGMENTS

As two individuals who came to the study of the movies from other disciplines, we would like to indicate our intellectual indebtedness to scholars such as Sol Worth, Andrew Tudor, Ian Jarvie, Thomas Guback, Denis McQuail, Herbert Gans, Robert Lewis Shayon, and Tom Carney. Research assistance for the first edition was provided by Jan Allison and Cal Moore, some advice on substantive issues by Mary Gerace Gold and Hugh Edmunds, and typing services by Doreen Truant.

During the protracted and laborious process involved in revising the original edition of this book, there were numerous individuals who provided assistance and support. We would like to thank: Mary Lynn Becker for diligently securing articles, information and data from a wide range of areas related to Chapters 1, 2 and 6 of the manuscript; Ann Gallant for cheerfully typing numerous inserts and revisions for Chapters 2 and 6, and for providing encouragement with her comment that she "found it all very interesting"; John Strick for supplying various materials related to the economics of the industry and helping to provide an economist's perspective for a noneconomist analyst; Sheila LaBelle for typing inserts and revisions for Chapter 1 while also helping its author to steer a course through the morass of academic administration; Hugh Edmunds for providing some background on recent developments in communications technologies; Jerry Edmonds for utilizing his computer skills to lay out a couple of the figures in the book; Rob Pearson for reviewing the original edition and suggesting sections that required updating and/or revision; Ann West for being exceedingly patient in shepherding these revisions through to completion; and Ev Dennis for being supportive of our efforts to make this volume as thorough and in-depth as limitations would allow.

In particular, Bruce Austin has been most encouraging in his support of the book in the past eight years, and was most generous in giving us an advanced look at his important study of film audiences — *Immediate Seating*. A special thank-you goes to The Gannett Center for Media Studies, which awarded Garth Jowett a generous residential fellowship for nine months, a small part of which provided the uninterrupted time for his portion of these revisions, and to Richard Simon of Goldman, Sachs & Co. and Syd Silverman of *Variety*, who graciously permitted us to reproduce materials from their reports and publications.

It is appealing to adopt George Gerbner's stance of apportioning blame to these individuals for any shortcomings in this volume, but clearly we alone must accept full responsibility should any such flaws exist. On the other hand, however, any successes must be shared at least in part with them.

AUTHORS' PREFACE
TO THE SECOND EDITION

Normally in any collaborative activity, the contribution of the collaborators is never exactly equivalent. In that respect, this volume can be considered entirely normal. While the project originated from Professor Jowett's interest in exploring the nature of movies as a medium of mass communication, he was concerned that his historical training and orientation would tend to overshadow other pertinent approaches. Hence the involvement of Professor Linton, who was responsible for the conceptualization and development of the overall framework of the volume on the basis of his background in political science and communications and his studies of production and viewing processes from a communication perspective. Within that framework, Professor Linton wrote Chapters 1, 2, and 6 and Professor Jowett Chapters 3, 4, and 5.

Despite this division of labor, this volume was an outgrowth of our mutual surprise and minor annoyance that movies were almost never included when discussions of the "mass" media arose. Since the publication of the first edition of this book in 1980, there have been some encouraging signs that movies are now being incorporated into academic discussions of the mainstream mass media. This is clearly evidenced by the fact that most of the introductory "media and society" textbooks now include a chapter on the movies, although there is still a tendency to position movies as a separate form of "entertainment," with a specialized audience. There is also a reluctance to consider the extensive interrelationships between movies and the other media, as we have tried to emphasize in this study.

Why movies should be treated so pristinely, and as a "special case," when small, local newspapers, magazines or radio stations are labeled as mass media is not clear, for the audience for a particular movie can number in the tens of millions. In 1980, this book therefore was modestly offered as an *initial* attempt to examine the movies as one segment of the mass communications infrastructure, and we continue to make no apologies for not adequately covering their role as an art. This aspect of film has received extensive coverage elsewhere, and in the last eight years many books on "movies as art" have been published. From our perspective, a few significant books on the inside workings of the film industry have been published which have proved to be insightful.

The limitations of space also require that we limit the extent of our discussion of certain topics, and we trust that readers will understand this. We also want to go on record as acknowledging that we both love movies, and this may have colored some of our perceptions; but our intentions are honorable, and we would hate to see the movies disappear, as has so often been predicted.

Finally, the preparation of the first edition of this book was a genuine learning experience for both of us, and the preparation of the second edition was no less so. The movie industry cannot be pinned to a board like a dead moth, to be studied at leisure. This book was technically obsolete the day after we prepared the manuscript, as the film makers are constantly searching for new ways to "make a deal." Jim Linton's chapters especially indicate the enormous changes in the entire movie industry since 1980. We thought that we knew something about movies until we started to assess them as a mass communications medium. Then we learned how little previous work had been done on this particular aspect of the movies, and we gained not only respect for the subject, but a valuable new perspective on the importance of movies as an integral institution in modern society.

Observing the movies since then and preparing this revised edition has only served to underscore that initial impression: we continue to be amazed at how much there is to learn and how quickly situations and conditions change. Two examples should suffice: Several companies producing video games entered and exited the corporate structure of the movie industry in the few short years before and after the onset of the 1980s. More profoundly, the penetration of the VCR in North America rose from a negligible level to over 50% in the period between the two editions of this book, and the role of video cassette sales and rentals had a similar impact on overall movie revenues.

What is probably even more remarkable, however, has been the theatrical movies' resilience in the face of such significant changes. Despite the phenomenal growth in alternative methods of exhibition, and the decrease in the number of people in the traditionally heavy moviegoing age groups of the population, the total theatrical audience for motion pictures has remained relatively stable over the last decade or so. Combined with steadily escalating ticket prices, this situation led to box office records being broken a number of times in the 1980s.

In fact, many movie industry insiders claim that the proliferation of home video has actually renewed interest in theatrical movies, explaining the revitalization at the box office. Some also note that theatrical box office performance determines a movie's value in subsequent markets (home video, pay cable, etc.). Such a contention would underscore our view that *theatrical* movies are not only an economic fulcrum in the motion picture business, but also a cultural one in the general media realm as well. The passing years have tended only to solidify and extend the movies' preeminent position among the various elements of mass-mediated culture, as the analysis of Chapter 1 attempts to demonstrate.

We will be watching the developments that take place in the rest of the 1980s and in the 1990s with great interest. And should there be a third edition of this particular overview of the movies, we anticipate there will be numerous significant changes that we will have to interpret and report. Although some additional erosion of the theatrical movie audience may be one such phenomenon, we remain confident that pronouncing the death of the theatrical motion picture altogether will not be required.

James M. Linton
Windsor, Ontario, Canada

Garth Jowett
Houston, Texas

1

A NEW PERSPECTIVE
Movies as Mass Communication

While writing about the movies began almost as soon as they were invented, serious study of them on a widespread basis didn't really occur until the mid-1960s. With much energy diverted to justifying the movies as a worthwhile aesthetic experience, the study of movies has advanced very slowly on only a piecemeal basis. There has also been little or no correlation of the findings produced by the various scholars who have utilized the methodologies of their diverse disciplines to study selected aspects of the movies. In approaching the movies as a process of communication and a medium that occupies a central role in mass-mediated culture, however, it is hoped that a better understanding of the movies can be achieved and the stage set for more fruitful studies in the future.

STUDYING THE MOVIES

Observers and analysts began writing about the movies and their role in society almost immediately after their invention. It was not until the 1960s and 1970s, however, that the study of movies captured the popular imagination, when large numbers of students enrolled in a plethora of film studies courses and programs which had suddenly sprung up on campuses around the world, most notably in the United States and Canada. This period also witnessed what Roger Manvell (1971) has called "the explosion of film studies," the almost exponential increase in books and articles on the subject of movies. If nothing else signaled the increased recognition of the importance of movies in cultural life, it was this phenomenal increase in the publication of books, for as Ernest Callenbach (1971:11) observed, "if anything signifies Seriousness, it is books."

Despite this growth in the interest in examining the movies, however, film study has remained "overexposed" and "underdeveloped." While much material has been produced, not much of it has generated truly meaningful insights about the nature of the movies and their role in society (one almost has to go back to the pioneering empirical and theoretical works of the 1910s, 1920s, and 1930s to find any); little has been written that suggests the connections among the various meaningful findings that have been produced, although Jarvie (1970) and Tudor (1974a) are two notable exceptions here; and only an insignificant number of works have provided a springboard for further study and research, as Guback (1969) did for the study of the economics of the movies. This situation has led some observers to question whether film study can (or even *should*) ever become a "field" or "discipline," despite the concerted efforts of some scholars to create one (Monaco, 1974).

Disciplines have typically been delineated by reference to their unique investigative method, by their concern with a specific subject, or by being tied to a specific purpose (Krippendorff, 1969). None of these approaches would seem to be entirely applicable to film study. Methodologies seem to be almost as numerous as the scholars and researchers active in the area (structuralism, semiology, Marxism, psychoanalysis, and humanism being but a few) and have often been a source of conflict, especially in the realm of aesthetics and criticism (see, for example, the exchange between Lovell, 1969, 1970, and Wood, 1969). Subject matter would seem to be a simple organizing principle, but here again differences of opinion about how or where to draw the boundary line are pronounced. De Antonio (1971) notes the shortsightedness of excluding from the category "films" those which are created primarily for exhibition on television, and Linton (1974) points out similar problems in eliminating videotape from the generic definition, especially in light of future technological developments in production and exhibition methods. Similarly, the criterion of purpose is also inapplicable as a result of its being inextricably linked to the previous two. In many ways, movies are being studied in a fashion similar to the examination of the elephant by Saxe's six blind men of Indostan — and with similar results!

There are numerous reasons for this dilemma, not the least of which is the relative recency of the endeavor. Despite the rather long history of writings on the movies, it is only since the mid-1960s that the movies have received widespread, serious attention. In addition, given that there has been no traditional disciplinary framework within which researchers and scholars interested in examining the movies have been trained, those who have pursued their study exhibit a great diversity of backgrounds. In the process of pursuing their investigations, then, these researchers have simply transferred the approaches, techniques, and methodologies of their original disciplines to the study of the movies. At various times, literary scholars, historians, aestheticians, philosophers, sociologists, psychologists, psychoanalysts, anthropologists, political scientists, and practitioners of other disciplines have undertaken research on different facets of the movies. Virtually none of this work has been done within a multidisciplinary, let alone an interdisciplinary, framework. Consequently, the fragmented nature of our knowledge about the movies is not without reason.

BEYOND THE MOVIES AS ART

The roots of this particular problem can be traced back almost to the origins of the motion picture itself and are related to the status of the movies in the mind of the public. To most people, movies were (and still are) a form of entertainment, pure and simple. While some people saw the movies as a harmless diversion, others saw them as crass escapism; in neither case did they consider the movies worthy of serious thought. At least one group, however, took the movies very seriously indeed. This latter group felt that the movies constituted an entirely new art form, and it was these people who were the original writers in the field. These partisans gave priority to boosting the movies as an art and to vindicating "movie-going . . . as a respectable activity for men of intellect and refinement" since movies were despised by cultured persons (Perkins, 1972:9). As a consequence, "Much of the effort which might have gone toward extending our understanding of the new medium has instead been poured into the bottomless pit of aesthetic respectability" (Tudor, 1974b:8).

This situation prompted Sol Worth (1971) to recommend that the movies be approached as a "non-art." Worth was not proposing that the movies could not be or were not necessarily works of art; however, he was convinced that the only fruitful approach to the study of film entailed examining movies as a medium and process of communication. He asserted:

> My objections to the older assumptions of art-non-art are based mainly on their exclusiveness and noncontinuity. While all art might be said to be communicative, all communication is most certainly not art. Assumptions that fail to provide criteria for the analysis of messages falling between the extremes of good and bad, beautiful and ugly and art and non-art must prove singularly unfit as basic assumptions for the analysis of films that so clearly fall between these extremes [Worth, 1971:183].

Tudor (1974b) has labeled these two basic contrasting orientations toward theories of film "models" and "aesthetics." The former are "aimed principally at scientific comprehension of [how] film [operates as a medium]," while the latter are "aimed at principally making evaluative judgements" (Tudor, 1974b:15). Most of the emphasis in the writing about movies has been in the area of aesthetics. The work that has been done in developing models of films has become increasingly narrow and specialized. The situation has changed drastically from one in which Eisenstein had intended "to create a mighty, overarching, scientific theory of film" (Tudor, 1974b:11). In the process of this narrowing of purpose, there has been a corresponding shift in concern from the movies themselves to "extra-cinematic" considerations (Tudor, 1974b). Many scholars and researchers are less interested in the movies per se than in some facet of human behavior linked to them — an approach Metz (1974) has labeled "filmology."

The intention of this particular volume, then, is to *approximate* one of Tudor's tasks for "maximal" theory: the reunification of these various elements so that one may gain a better understanding of how theatrical movies operate, of the position they occupy in society, and of the kinds of "effects" they can have on individuals and the social order. In doing so, it is necessary to delineate the territory that will be covered and to clarify some terms that will be employed.

First, this study is more interested in "movies" than "films." While these two terms have been used almost interchangeably up to this point, there are some profound differences in their connotations which have relevance for our purpose. As John Simon (1971) has observed, "To call film movies is . . . to view it as an entertainment rather than as an art." While the two terms are not mutually exclusive, there is a fundamental difference in approach between movies which attempt to provide enjoyment and relaxation, and films which attempt to convey enlightenment through challenge and involvement. The former approach is the much more common one, given the high level of funding involved in production. Audiences must be attracted to provide revenue to cover costs and provide a return on investment, and this is done by "giving the people what they want." While art may be the result of such a quest, it is more a by-product of the process than a primary focus.

Admittedly, this is a somewhat superficial explanation of the dynamics of movie financing and economics and fails to account for the continuing existence of what might be termed "art films." These matters are explored in more detail, however, in Chapter 2. Suffice it to say at this point that the focus of this study will be primarily theatrical movies that are designed to entertain and that constitute the vast majority of moviegoing experiences for the citizens of North America and the rest of the world.

A MODEL OF MOVIES AS COMMUNICATION

In taking this approach, then, we are examining movies as a facet of mass culture and mass art — or as one type of "mass-mediated culture." The concept of mass-mediated culture has been defined by Michael Real (1977:14) as encompassing "expressions of culture as they are received from contemporary mass media, whether they arise from elite, folk, popular, or mass origins," and is based on the assumption that "all culture when transmitted by mass media becomes in effect popular culture." Movies are popular culture in the sense that their appeal depends on a skillful combination of familiarity and novelty (Gans, 1957) and often involves a certain degree of empathy between the audience and the creator, with much of the latter's success depending on personal "style" (Real, 1977). In many other instances, however, movies are mass culture products since they are designed to please the average taste of an undifferentiated audience. As with the other media, the pervasiveness of the movies (both nationally and internationally), the nature of the messages they convey, and the role that they occupy in the overall cultural system make them significant objects deserving of attention and requiring a multidisciplinary or interdisciplinary perspective to be fully understood (Real, 1977).

The movies are messages generated within a filmic communication system, then, and a full understanding of their nature, function, and effects requires an approach that focuses on the movies as a *process* of communication. A model of this process in Figure 1.1, is designed to elaborate on the intricacies of the various stages. This model is basically an expansion of the components of the classic communication model in which a source conveys a message via some medium to a receiver, who responds in some fashion. Some modifications of its terms are included to make it more germane to this particular communication system. For example, the generic "source" has been divided into three segments (producer, distributor, and exhibitor), and, partly as a consequence of that division, the number of feedback loops (that is, the responses of the receiver to the source) has been increased substantially.

The model employs many of the standard divisions or stages of the movie-making/movie-viewing or filmic communication process, but also attempts to amplify the often neglected *linkages* or *connections* among these various divisions or stages. Economic studies of the movies, for example, have noted the strains toward vertical integration of the production/distribution/exhibition stages of the process. In order to have a fuller understanding of the dynamics of these stages and of how they relate to the *kind* of movies that are produced, however, it is first necessary to locate these stages within a social/cultural/political milieu. It also helps to realize that the nature of the uncertainty about audience preferences (as measured by box office receipts) necessitates the development of an often vague "audience image" that governs much of the decision-making in the economic stages of the process (Gans, 1957). Similarly, much of what has been written about the "effects" of movies has ignored the nature of the viewing process and the question of how movies function as a symbolic or semiotic system of communication. By focusing on movies as both the product of and raw material for different but interrelated stages of the overall process of communication, it is hoped that a more holistic view of the movies will emerge.

THE MOVIES' PLACE IN MASS CULTURE

Beyond creating that understanding, there is also a concern in demonstrating the movies' connections with the other facets of massmediated culture — such as publishing, television, and recorded music — and to indicate the role which movies play within the "mass media mix" in society. Since the advent of television, movies have not been perceived as the major social force they once were. The displacement by television of movies' role as the most important entertainment medium (as measured by the absolute numbers reached and by the number of different demographic categories of the popu-

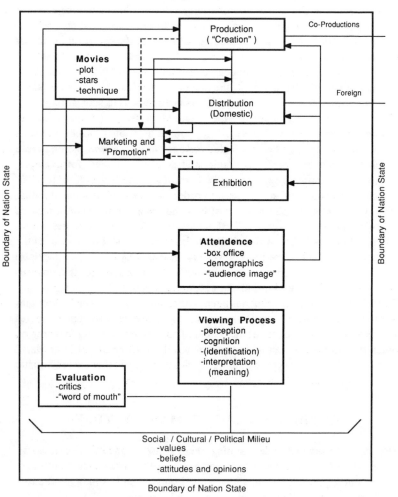

Figure 1.1. A Model of Theatrical Movies as a Process of Communication

lation attracted) has caused us to devalue movies' functions and influence. This attitude neglects the fact that movies are literally larger than life, are attended at one time or another by all segments of society, have immense appeal to a particular age group in society (adolescents and young adults), and occupy a special place in the social ritual of this segment of the populace at a time when they are establishing patterns for the rest of their lives.

In addition, the movies have a longer and more glamorous history than most of the other forms of mass-mediated culture, and more of an aura of art about them — in spite of the fact that creating art is not the major objective of movie-making. The allure of prestige and status which movies confer is demonstrated by the fact that rock stars (the reigning deities of popular culture) attempt to make the transition to movie stardom, for example Rod Stewart, Elton John, and David Bowie in the 1970s (Levine, 1979) and Sting, Prince and Madonna in the 1980s. The attraction is so strong that in the late 1980s Tina Turner contemplated forsaking her singing career to become an actress. This central position of the movies in mass-mediated cultural life means that they are both the source for and the anticipated destination of many other forms of mass culture. An attempt has been made to present these relationships in Figure 1.2.

In line with McLuhan's (1966) dictum that the structure of one medium becomes the content of the medium that follows it, movies have drawn very heavily on literary works as source material — more specifically, on the novel's narrative fiction approach, and on stage plays, novellas, short stories, and nonfiction to a lesser extent. So strong is this link that film production companies are willing to pay huge sums for the movie rights for best-selling novels — or even for prospective bestsellers. Books are so important to the movie industry that studio story editors have come to occupy crucial positions, and there have even been instances in which companies have purchased the rights to a book before it has been written, the "property" consisting solely of an outline (Tripp, 1979). The major studios (Metro-Goldwyn-Mayer and Twentieth Century-Fox) have also bankrolled novelists. By providing a modest "up front" payment and the promise of a more substantial sum upon publication, the studio secured the movie rights to the unwritten novel. While the studio also had to pay bonuses if the book made *The New York Times* bestseller list and was committed to using the novelist to write the screenplay, this arrangement gave the moviemaker the advantage of direct access to potentially best-selling material at prices well below the going rates for established best-selling novels (Windsor *Star,* 1979a). In the early 1980s Paramount developed a similar arrangement for stage productions. Through Paramount Theatre Productions they provided the Chicago-based The Apollo Group with $500,000 to mount nine original works. In return, Paramount had the right to take any of the productions to Broadway and eventually make it into a movie if they so desired (Windsor *Star,* 1983).

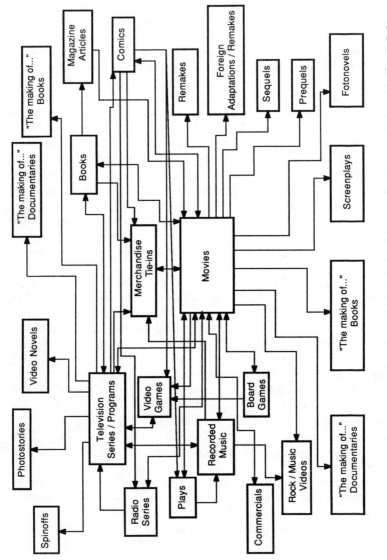

Figure 1.2. The Movies' By-Products and Their Relationship to Other Forms of Mass-Mediated Culture

Conversely, movies that are produced from original screenplays are often novelized for the book market after their successful release—or in some instances at the same time, to capitalize on the double-barreled publicity. In the mid-1980s, the novelization of the Brian DePalma updated remake of the 1932 Paul Muni vehicle, *Scarface,* involved a different twist: the paperback version came out five months *before* the scheduled release of the movie. Using clips from the movie in television ads and the face of star Al Pacino on the cover of the book, the paperback reached the top 20 best-seller list within a month of its publication. In addition to earning substantial returns itself, the book generated the kind of awareness and hype that Hollywood loves to see for the movie version (Chadwick, 1983).

Movies also spawn screenplays, books describing the making of the movies, comic book adaptations, and a more recent development in movie publishing—the fotonovel. This is a kind of photographic comic book in which the panels consist of photographs rather than drawings, although the characters "speak" via the standard "balloons" of normal comics. Such publications have long been popular in Europe as the romantic fantasy photo-novel, its TV-inspired variants being labeled "photostories" and "video novels." These publications do not seem to have become a widespread phenomenon and may possibly be reserved for those movies geared to viewers attracted to teen fan magazines, i.e., mainly adolescent and preadolescent girls. Employed for the right movie, however, they do have the potential to be quite successful: for example, the *Grease Fotonovel* sold over one million copies (at $2.50 each) by the end of 1978 after having been published that summer at about the same time the movie was released (Clarke, 1978).

In addition, documentaries and two- to six-minute "featurettes" are often made about the production of movies and are offered free to the television networks for the exposure. Sometimes they are purchased by the networks if the movie has already established itself and can be expected to attract viewers, as happened in the case of *Star Wars* when it was rereleased (Buck, 1978). Although some such productions have become classics in their own right (such as the one documenting the creation of Steven Spielberg's *Raiders of the Lost Ark*), most of these efforts are readily identifiable as "program-length commercials" disguised as documentaries (O'Connor, 1987).

Movies also recycle themselves in the form of sequels (*The Color of Money, Beverly Hills Cop II, Jaws IV—Rocky∞!*), remakes (*Scarface, The Fly, Little Shop of Horrors*), and beginning with *Butch and Sundance: The Early Days*, the "prequel." The mid-to late 1980s also saw the rise of the Americanized adaptation/remake of successful foreign (especially French) films: *Down and Out In Beverly Hills, The Man With One Red Shoe, Three Men and a Baby.* Television series are often based on some reworking of a successful movie: *Happy Days* (from *American Graffiti*) and *M*A*S*H* are just two examples—albeit two of the most successful. "Translations" from television series to movies are much less frequent; the *Star Trek* movies are notable exceptions. The late 1980s, however, saw plans to produce a spate of such movies derived from old TV series such as *Dragnet* and *The Flintstones,* based on an attempt to appeal to adults, who had seen the originals as children, and to children who were familiar with them through promotional materials and syndicated reruns (Harmetz, 1987). The move by CBS and ABC into the production of theatrical movies could have accentuated this encroachment by television into the movies' sphere had the ventures not failed. Among other things, this arrangement would have ensured that the two networks had movies to run on TV after their theatrical release.

Movies and comic books have shown a great affinity for one another, especially in the late 1970s. Marvel Comics produced one-shot "Marvel Movie Specials" of *2001, A Space Odyssey, The Island of Dr. Moreau, Logan's Run,* and *The Deep* (Stackhouse, 1978). While these were produced in regular format and, with the exception of *2001,* were tied to the release of the movies, *Close Encounters of the Third Kind* was released as a large-format "Marvel Superspecial" and *Star Wars* was turned into a continuing comic book series, the first six issues of which were reprinted in both a large format "Marvel Treasury" edition and a Ballantine paperback version. The trend continued in the 1980s for movies such as *Alien, Labyrinth, House II,* and *Robocop* (among others). In the other direction, the phenomenal box office success of *Superman* in the 1970s initiated the production of movie versions of such comic book standards as Popeye, Flash Gordon, Little Orphan Annie, and Sheena, Queen of the Jungle (Beller, 1979). Despite the lackluster results of these movies, plus the disappointing boxoffice performances of *Supergirl* and *Howard the Duck,* films based upon the exploits of comic book heroes are likely to be a featured genre in the next decade. This development was ensured by the phenomenal success of the movie *Batman,* which took in more than $100 million in the first ten days of its release, after an unprecedented publicity buildup which centered on whether or not a motion picture could faithfully capture the essence of the fabled "Dark Knight." Obviously movie audiences as well as the comic book fans were happy with the final production. As a result, other projects involving comic book heroes, most notably *Dick Tracy* starring Warren Beatty, were immediately put into production.

More rarely, movies are translated into radio series, as was the case with the phenomenally successful *Star Wars* (Toronto Globe and Mail, 1979) and later *The Empire Strikes Back.* However, recorded music is another matter. The increased spending on records, cassettes — and now compact discs — in recent years (despite the setback in 1979) has caused movie marketers to put increased emphasis on selling movie soundtracks, and this strategy has been highly profitable in many instances. In the 1970s, for example, dollar sales of the *Saturday Night Fever* soundtrack outdistanced the film's box office for its initial release, and the *Sgt. Pepper* soundtrack album garnered $56 million worth of advance orders before the movie was even released! (This, of course, follows on the Beatles' original version made more than ten years before.)

The 1980s saw the success of soundtracks consisting of oldies, such as *The Big Chill,* and new songs, such as *Footloose* and *Top Gun.* During the decade, movies paid increasing attention to the role of music, and in some instances attempted to intermingle period and contemporary songs. *Dirty Dancing* was an extremely successful example, bringing in box office receipts of about $57 million by the end of 1987 (against a production cost of under $6 million), and having its soundtrack on *Billboard's* album chart for five weeks, with anticipated sales of over three million units that year (Holden, 1987). In late 1988 *Dirty Dancing* completed the "cycle" by also becoming a weekly, albeit shortlived, television series.

This was also the period in which the movies (along with the rest of society) discovered music/rock videos. *Flashdance* is acknowledged as the break-through in using this form of "invisible marketing" (Harmetz, 1983b), with some 200 video cassettes containing five songs being provided to the most frequented dance clubs in 60 major cities. The popularity of cable channels such as MTV in the USA and MuchMusic in Canada, and the explosion of video programs on conventional television provided a major outlet to access traditionally hard-to-reach teenagers with materials which have all the adver-tising elements of a theatrical trailer but are not perceived as an advertisement by the audience (Janusonis, 1986; Windsor *Star,* 1986c). Since the videos can promote the movie soundtrack, as well as the movie itself—and if there are enough popular ones from a single movie, they can be packaged for sale directly—music videos can be expected to grow in number and influence in movie marketing.

The ancillary rights to a movie can be sold, resulting in the production of merchandise tie-ins: toys, games, T-shirts, posters, lunch-buckets, glassware, sunglasses, cookies—and in the case of *The Swarm* even "bee helmets." A large part of the appeal to producers, of the comic-book-derived movies mentioned above, may be their potential for this sale of related merchandise. Character toys, for example, constituted 20% of one Canadian toy manufacturer's stock in the late 1970s having risen from about two percent a decade earlier (Windsor *Star,* 1979d). Despite the general popularity of such tie-ins, the greater risk involved in achieving movie success and the repetition and ease of access afforded by television mean TV characters are favored by toy companies. In fact, the bad merchandising experiences afforded by such movies as *Gremlins* and *Annie* caused buyers for toy retailers in the mid-1980s to rank movie-based dolls behind both TV show-based ones and Disney-type characters in terms of profitability (Ratliff, 1986). This fact may at least have saved us from the situation in which movies are created solely as vehicles to sell toys, as has been the case with such TV programs as *GoBots, Transform-ers, Masters of the Universe* and *She-Ra,* according to some critics and commentators—although there have been movies made from such TV fare as the *GoBots* and *Care Bears* (Price, 1986), as well as *He-Man* and *Masters of the Universe.*

Video games burst onto the scene in the early 1980s, and although their pervasiveness and impact waned rather quickly, they did manage to establish themselves as an important leisure product, and the movies were an obvious source of raw material. Science fiction was a particularly attractive subject, with the inevitable games based on the *Star Wars* movies and characters, and others drawing upon such movies as *E.T., Alien, Superman, Krull,* and *Fantastic Voyage.* The venerable old board game, which more frequently owed its origin to a movie than vice versa, turned the tables in 1985, inspiring a movie version of *Clue* — complete with three alternate endings exhibited at different locations across the country. It, too, had been adapted as a video game prior to the move's release.

Finally — and the least encouraging development in "cross-overs" according to many movie critics — was a movie produced in the late 1980s based on a character from a television commercial (Belkin, 1987). This was a vehicle for Jim Varney who had appeared in more than 2,600 advertisements in 140 television markets between 1980 and 1987, selling products ranging from Toyotas to sour cream. As character Ernest P. Worall, his trademark was annoying his unseen neighbor ("Hey Vern") with unsolicited and unappreciated advice. With a fan club of 20,000 and licensed products from T-shirts to beach towels, a movie was the next logical step. Hated by the critics, but loved by the young moviegoing public, *Ernest Goes to Camp* earned more than $11 million in its first two weeks of release, surpassed only by *Beverly Hills Cop II* for the same period of time. Varney completed the mass culture cycle with a successful Saturday morning show, *Hey, Vern, It's Ernest!,* and appeared in a fall 1988 sequel, *Ernest Saves Christmas* — which did relatively good box office business.

Obviously, then, the movies are firmly entrenched in the economic and industrial complex that produces our mass-mediated culture. These numerous connections with other forms of mass culture which the movies exhibit can be partially explained by the corporate linkages of the companies that produce them. For example, Paramount is controlled by the conglomerate Gulf and Western, which in 1987 also controlled 470 U.S. theaters through the Festival, Trans-Lux, and Mann chains (although it was selling 50% to Warner Communications) and had an interest in the Canadian Famous Players theater chain; owned Madison Square Gardens and the New York Knicks; and held 50% of the USA Network. Columbia was owned by the Coca-Cola Co. which also had interests in radio stations and merchandising endeavors, and had merged Columbia Pictures and Tri-Star Pictures to create Columbia Pictures Entertainment Inc. Ted Turner reversed the movie-studio-buys-television-stations trend in 1986 when his Turner Broadcasting System acquired MGM-UA Entertainment. He quickly sold the company's movie and television operations back to Kirk Kerkorian, retaining the rights to MGM's 3,000-title film library and scandalizing movie-lovers by colorizing the original black-and-white movies to appeal to an audience accustomed to color TV. Twentieth

Century-Fox had been bought by Rupert Murdoch's News Corporation Ltd. and added to his stable of seven U.S. television stations, Fox Broadcasting, and other publishing and broadcasting properties in the U.S. and abroad. Similar arrangements held for virtually all the other majors in the movie industry: Disney, MGM/United Artists, Universal and Warner Bros. (Harmetz, 1988b). They were, in effect, all embedded in, or in and of themselves, mass culture empires.

This is the reason that the movies require serious attention and comprehensive examination at all stages of the communication process. It is only by tracing movies from their inception right through to their diffusion into the social/cultural/political milieu, and by linking these stages to each other, that we will come to understand the way the movies function in our lives and the extent to which they influence us individually and as a society. In the chapters that follow, then, an attempt has been made to chart the broad outline of such an overview.

2

"WHAT YOU SEE IS WHAT YOU GET"
The Economics of the Movies

The movies are a business enterprise which is governed by the primary goal of all businesses: making money. The unpredictability of the future preferences of moviegoers, however, makes movies a business subject to much more risk than many other industries. Faced with this uncertainty, moviemakers have generated an implicit philosophy or ideology about moviemaking which provides them with an image of their audience and their viewing interests. This "audience image" has tended to narrow the range of subject matter and forms that movies employ, and has caused moviemakers to invoke formulaic approaches and engage in imitations of "breakthrough" successes, in what are known as movie "cycles." As innovations are introduced and the environment changes, the "landscape" of the industry adapts, with the "chameleon-like" majors managing to maintain dominance in the marketplace.

MOVIES AND THE GOALS OF BUSINESS

The making and screening of movies is primarily a business enterprise based on the industrial model — despite the overtones (or some might say pretensions) of art alluded to in Chapter 1. The economic portion of the filmic communication process presented in Figure 1.1 is composed of the three basic components of the industrial model in modern societies. The movie production segment corresponds to manufacturing, the distribution segment to wholesaling, and the exhibition segment to retailing (Larmett et al., 1978).

An additional component which has come to occupy an important position in modern business endeavors is marketing and promotion, and these activities have played an increasingly important role in the movie business as well. In some instances, these functions have become so important that advertising campaigns cost as much as the actual production of the movie itself, and "some recent marketing campaigns have cost as much as twice the negative cost [that is, the cost to produce the movie]" (Larmett et al., 1978:8). Rather than being a role that is adopted by a distinct entity, however, marketing and promotion are normally handled by a special division of the distribution company or "contracted out" to a firm which specializes in such activities. While the distributor usually has the formative role in designing the marketing campaign for a movie, there are situations in which an influential producer will contribute input, as will exhibitors (Drabinsky, 1976). In the case of exhibitors, such input normally occurs at the local level when the costs of advertising are being shared between the distributor and the exhibitor.

Since business is the primary orientation of the movies, the primary goal and value of the movie enterprise is not unexpectedly that of business in general — that is, the making of money. There are those like William Fadiman (1973), however, who would reject such a crass assertion. Writing from the perspective of the phenomenal decline of Hollywood in the late 1960s and early 1970s, Fadiman (1973:5) contends that movie-making is a "business which is at the same time an art and an industry." As such, Fadiman feels, it is beyond the understanding of the operators of the conglomerates who were then beginning to buy up the movie production studios and attempting to completely industrialize an activity that involves the "creation" of essentially unique commodities.

As support for this contention, there is evidence that United Artists had experienced some difficulty working within the Transamerica organization (Schuyten, 1978) — with disgruntled executives finally breaking away to form Orion Pictures and UA eventually being bought by MGM to become part of MGM/UA Communication Inc. Troubled Columbia Pictures changed owners three times during the 1970s and early 1980s, and in the late 1980s, Coca-Cola Co. merged it with Tri-Star Pictures to form Columbia Pictures Entertainment Inc., cutting its own share in the venture to 49% (Groer, 1987). Despite such difficulties within the conglomerate structures, some of the majors still have managed to produce at least the occasional commercial and critical success, indicating that this form of ownership might not be completely inimical to the creative aspects of movie-making. By choosing studio executives who are empathetic to the movie industry and knowledgeable in its ways, the corporate leaders behind Paramount (Harwood, 1988) and Disney/Touchstone (Koepp, 1988) have managed to achieve considerable success. Nevertheless, Fadiman's claims and those similar to it would seem to ignore the fact that movies have long been subject to the dictates of the financial interests in society due to the comparatively large sums of money that have been required for their production (Cochran, 1975). As Janet Wasko (1982) points out, even D. W. Griffith, revered for his contribution to the growth of the movies as an art, was involved with banks and other financial institutions:

He had helped create a new American art-form, but he had also contributed to the growth of motion pictures as a new American industry with commercial considerations and restrictions similar to any other capitalist enterprise. [p. 41].

THE EFFECTS OF UNCERTAINTY

There are certain strains in Fadiman's argument, however, that bear closer examination since they have important implications for the economics of movie-making. One of these claims is that each movie, while mass produced, is essentially a *unique* commodity; the second is that the operation of the movie-making process defies order and demands constant risk-taking. The first factor translates into economics as "a high degree of product differentiation" which results in promotional competition rather than admission price competition (Larmett et al., 1978). The second characteristic is described in economic terminology as "demand uncertainty," and combined with the first factor means that "the larger producers would tend toward restrictive trade practices in an attempt to gain control and establish some 'oligopolistic order' in the market" (Strick, 1978:409). These factors account for the early tendency toward vertical (producer-distributor-exhibitor) integration in the movie industry before it was disallowed by the U.S. Supreme Court in 1948. They also account for the continuing struggle between the major producer-distributors on the one hand and the independent producers and the exhibitors (including the various outlets afforded by the new communications technologies) on the other.

These two factors in combination also have profound and far-reaching implications for the more fundamental matter of the way people involved in the movies conceptualize the very nature and operation of the movie-making endeavor, which in turn has a very significant impact on the manner in which they operate. The measure of success in movie-making is attendance, either in terms of the number of admissions, the dollar value of box office receipts, or the dollar value of rental fees which exhibitors return to the distributor. (While each of these can be considered an indicator of success, in the pragmatic business arena, admissions are not very helpful in gauging financial gain. Box office figures may be useful in the early stages of release to signal a movie's initial impact under specific circumstances, but it is the rentals which the distributor receives that are used in calculating actual profit or loss [Daly, 1980].) The problem with these measurements (which they share with television ratings) is that they are determined after the fact, do not explain why people attend movies, and consequently are lacking in predictive value. Popularity in the past has been found to be no guarantee of success in the future.

Some attempts have been made to develop more sophisticated techniques to anticipate audience interests. Handel (1950) has provided the most extensive catalogue of such efforts. It should be noted, however, that such investigations were given publicity only in the late 1940s and early 1950s — a time when the movie industry was reeling from the loss of attendance occasioned by the introduction of television. At most other times, data from, and even the very existence and nature of, the industry's research on their product is treated as secretively as the data on various facets of the industry (Daly, 1980; Strick, 1978). The major exceptions would seem to be the studies of America's moviegoing habits conducted by the Opinion Research Corporation for the Motion Picture Association of America (see Motion Picture Association of America [MPAA], 1987).

There have been various tests of stories, casts and casting combinations, the appeal and comprehension of individual scenes and events, and titles, not to mention the tried and perhaps not so true "sneak previews" (Handel, 1950). There are also organizations such as Emotional Response Index Systems, Incorporated (ERIS) which claims it can predict the ultimate success of a proposed movie just by analyzing the *script* against the emotional reactions (as measured by Galvanic Skin Response) of a 7,000-person sample gathered several years ago (Scott, 1978). The "bottom line," however, is that it has been estimated that a low percentage of movies is successful (that is, returns a profit): director Sidney Lumet estimates it at one in four (cited in Edmunds and Strick, 1977); while MPAA President Jack Valenti, puts it at one in five, with one in three losing money (cited in Daly, 1980). Peter S. Myers (1983:283) contends that, "As a matter of record, only two out of ten motion pictures show a profit or break even." Suzanne Mary Donahue (1987:32) seems to have the most complicated version of this Hollywood "rule of thumb":

> It is generally believed that seven out of ten pictures lose money, two out of ten break even and one is a huge success, or that two out of three pictures do not generate enough revenue to pay for prints or ads, with less [sic] than one out of three pictures making more than $10 million in film rentals.

It has also been observed that "There is no simple, consistent relationship between film themes, costs of production and box office receipts" (Edmunds and Strick, 1977:96). It would seem to be the case, then, that either (a) the wrong kind of research or not enough of it is being done, (b) sufficient and properly focused research is being conducted inadequately, or (c) the reliable and valid results of adequate research are being ignored or misinterpreted.

According to Thomas Simonet (1978a), however, the problem would appear to be even more deep-seated than the above explanations would suggest. In discussing the failure of Gallup's attempt in the 1940s to determine box office potential on the basis of the marquee values of movie performers, Simonet (1978a:8) concludes that the limited predictive utility of the marquee values is likely the result of "the inability of respondents to predict reliably their own future actions . . . [with them] tend[ing] to report as predictions what they wish they had done already or what in fact has satisfied them in the past" (italics added). In light of this conundrum, there is little wonder that movie executives are reduced to "reading box office tea leaves" (Madsen, 1975:153).

THE CREATION OF AN "AUDIENCE IMAGE"

In the face of this inability to predict successfully the future wishes of moviegoers or to predict them only to a limited extent (at this point in time, at least), the operators of the movie industry are forced to develop a "mental image of the anticipated or desired audience" (McQuail, 1969b), what Gans (1957) had earlier labeled "audience image." (Communication theorists contend that this "anticipatory feedback" is required in all communication situations, but it is more crucial in conditions of high uncertainty such as this.) This audience image functions as a foil against which the producer "unconsciously tests his product even while he is creating it" (Gans, 1957:316). This image is not a unified concept, however. The potential movie audience, while composed of unique individuals, is grouped into diverse "publics," each of which is an aggregate of people who are seeking similar satisfactions from a movie. The moviemaker must sort through these various groups and evolve an audience image for *each specific movie.* The numerous impressions which constitute such an image are largely latent or internalized, and there is very little possibility of completely verifying the nature and composition of the publics for any particular movie. As a result, the numerous impressions constituting the audience image are often contradictory (Gans, 1957), and some are perhaps even imaginary (McQuail, 1969b).

The audience images of decisionmakers in the various phases of production (scriptwriter, producer, director, and so on) vie for dominance, and status in the industry depends on how successful previous decisions have been. The fickleness of the audience means, however, that one must validate and prove one's audience image each time out, hence the saying: "You're only as good as your *next* picture." The fact that these competing audience images cannot be tested before the movie is released means that "decisions may be made on the basis of irrelevant, but enforceable criteria" (Gans, 1957:322). The division of the movie business into the production, distribution, and exhibition segments also tends to distance further the creative personnel from their ultimate target — the audience. Jarvie (1970:42) aptly describes the situation that existed once this particular division of labor in the industry had been formalized:

> [The] artists were controlled by what the producers *thought,* the producers were controlled by what the distributors *thought* (or what the producers expected the distributors would *think*), the distributors were controlled by what they *thought* the cinema owners *thought* and the cinema owners were controlled by what they *thought* the audience wanted.

In light of all these complexities, moviemakers tend to engage in a form of *ritualism* — described by the famous sociologist Robert Merton as a device to allay anxieties by engaging in "routinized action." Applied to the media, it entails clinging to well-tried formulas with "known" audience appeal

(McQuail, 1969b); hence the tendency to minimize risks, for "cycles" to dominate (in other words, for there to be imitations of successful movie themes and formats) and for moviemakers to look to the successes of other media for inspiration, and vice versa, as evidenced in the situation presented in Figure 1.2.

Despite the rhetoric of "giving the people what they want," moviemakers establish the parameters of choice by determining the types of movies that will be produced, and this range of choice is conditioned by a conception of audience preferences that is based on a set of beliefs that generally lacks empirical support and probably cannot be completely disproved. Edmunds and Strick (1977) demonstrated, for example, that there was an increasing incidence of violent or otherwise "exploitive" movies during the late 1960s and early 1970s. They cited evidence of the dramatic increase in X-rated and Restricted movies during that period in the United States and Canada. This choice of content, they contended, was based on the belief that such themes were "safe" since people wanted to see them, despite the fact that a perusal of *Variety's* "All-Time Box-Office Champion Films" demonstrated a *fairly* large variety of "popular" themes. In addition, examination of the production costs and rentals to distributors of a sample of movies produced during the mid-1970s revealed: "The matter of whether the film depicts violence or nonviolence does not appear to be crucial to the success of the film" (Edmunds and Strick, 1977:84).

THE INDUSTRY'S "ARTICLES OF FAITH"

In order to understand fully the basis on and the manner in which decisions are made in the movie industry, it is necessary that we have as complete a picture of the industry's values and beliefs as possible. This requires that we examine and state the implicitly held tenets of the rather vague and amorphous framework of the "philosophy" or "ideology" of the movie industry. Such conventional wisdom or "articles of faith" about movies would consist of the following:

(1) The movies are a commercial enterprise and the various segments of the industry require an adequate return on investment in order for the system to continue to exist. (As observed above, however, not every movie is expected to make a profit. Nevertheless, there must be sufficient expectation of an *opportunity* for an adequate return on investment if investors are to be attracted [Edmunds and Strick, 1977].)

(2) Given the relatively high costs of production, movies simply cannot make an adequate return on the home market exclusively, especially in countries with a small population base, such as Canada. Movies are an international business, then, and successful themes are ones that tap uni-

versal concerns, there being little room for inward-looking movies that act as a form of national self-expression (Canadian Motion Picture Distributors Association, 1979).

(3) In order to attract people, movies must mirror public tastes and comply with the demands of the public (Fadiman, 1973).

(4) The numbers of people necessary to maintain the financial viability of movies can only be attracted by "entertainment." Entertainment is felt to be achievable only with movies which divert and provide escape; those which require too much serious thought and are too similar to real-life situations are to be avoided (Linton, 1978; Litwak, 1986).

(5) The average moviegoer is rather juvenile in his needs and interests (Fadiman, 1973). These needs and interests include: voyeurism, sadomasochism, sentimentality, levity, and excitement. These needs can be fulfilled by sex, violence, romance, comedy, and adventure, respectively.

(6) However base these needs or interests could be considered, they must be catered to in a manner which masks the fact that they are not noble, so that the moviegoer is not embarrassed, or so that his self-esteem is not diminished. "Successful films require a very special and often rare, combination of insight, taste and creativity" (Canadian Motion Picture Distributors Association, 1979:61). As Metz (1975) points out, since people are not coerced into attending movies, movies must provide people with an overall pleasurable experience if they are to be successful (financially).

(7) Stars play a large part in helping the audience fulfill these various fantasy needs, and the star system is one of Hollywood's most sacrosanct institutions (Fadiman, 1973).

(8) No matter what the subject matter or style of a particular movie, it has no effect on the viewer because entertainment is believed to be an innocent, socially neutral, harmless, value-free, and uninfluential experience (Linton, 1978).

(9) Movies are in competition with other forms of leisure activity (especially television) for the consumer's time and money. In light of that fact, they must provide what those other forms cannot provide. In the case of competition from television, they must also overcome the fact that the entertainment material is "free" (Edmunds and Strick, 1977; Fadiman, 1973). It is also noted that "the theatrical feature film industry is not a growth sector of the leisure time industry" (Canadian Motion Picture Distributors Association, 1979:59). The belief has been that such "uniqueness" is to be created through more sensational treatment of taboo subject matter (sex and violence) than is possible in the home, by providing popular stars who do not appear frequently on television (if at all), and through technological innovations that play on the nature of the movie medium and channel (image size, 3-D, cinemascope, special effects, and the like). More recently there have been attempts to convince the potential viewer that

seeing a particular movie is a social event of such magnitude that missing it would reduce one to the level of social misfit or "untouchable."

(10) The principal form for treating the subject matter of the movies is the closed, fictional, dramatic narrative in which "all the elements of the narrative have been drawn together, all questions arising from the film have been answered, and all situations presented in the film have been resolved by the time of its conclusion" (Linton and Jowett, 1977:479). The relationship that such a form establishes between the viewer and the movie allows the often contradictory demands of the moviegoing situation (see points 5 and 6 above) to be satisfied with a minimal amount of fuss and displeasure.

This set of beliefs and values contains some that can be considered true. From the work of Berlyne (1971), for example, it would be possible to suggest that the combination of certain subject matters and the narrative form would probably provide the conditions of complexity-simplicity and novelty-familiarity that would maximize hedonic value or pleasure. In addition, it is also probably true that, unless other financing sources were located (such as government subsidy), failure to attract a sufficient audience would lead to the ultimate demise of the movie industry. Others are contradictory, such as the requirement to fulfill baser "juvenile" needs and at one and the same time the desire to be "tasteful." Some are questionable, if not downright false, for example, the belief that entertainment has no impact and apparently exists outside the entire social process. There can be little doubt, however, that these various beliefs and values serve to support the basic goal and value of the movies' profit-making organizations, at times offering prescriptions and at others offering rationales for particular courses of action. Taken together they present a useful background against which a more detailed and systematic account of the economics of the movie industry can be undertaken.

MARKET POTENTIAL, PRODUCTION COSTS, AND FUNDING

According to Drabinsky (1976), there are three basic "tests" that a movie proposal must "pass" before the financing of its production can be contemplated seriously. The first of these is market potential: the ability of the movie to attract sufficient numbers of patrons to make the movie a profitable venture. As seen above, the uncertainty surrounding this speculation makes it a tricky matter at best and creates conditions which tend to constrain innovation, generating reliance on a limited number of formulas considered "safe" and leading to imitation of "breakthrough" successes. If it is projected that the proposed movie will have sufficient audience appeal, a second consideration is the availability of people of sufficient quality to make the movie. If the movie appears to be a good idea, but what are deemed to be the appropriate people (stars and directors, among others) are not available to make it, the sources of funding will not be forthcoming. If the movie passes these first two tests, it still must be demonstrated that the movie's proposed budget is reasonable. As Drabinsky (1976:121) points out, "Some pictures are just too expensive for anyone to make anymore" — although escalating average production costs and the enormous budgets of some individual movies would seem to undercut this particular observation.

This final consideration of budget is assessed in relation to the initial consideration of potential audience appeal (Edmunds and Strick, 1977). It must be remembered that the movie investor's goal is to maximize his investment. This goal can be achieved either by attempting to maximize the potential appeal of the movie, in which case costs are less of a concern, or attempting to minimize the costs of production, in which case the extent of box office draw is less of a concern. From this perspective, then, both the "blockbuster" and the smaller, more specialized movie are viable production approaches *as long as the viewer/cost ratio is maximized.* But, in fact, the latter may be more attractive to investors since several "lesser" films could be made for the same total investment as for one blockbuster, but the risk factor would be spread and reduced (Edmunds and Strick, 1977).

The costs involved in movie production are many and varied. The allocation of monies among the various categories for an average movie is as follows: sets and other physical properties, 35%; stars and cast, 20%; studio overhead, 20%; net profit after taxes, 10%; story costs, 5%; production and direct costs, 5%; and income taxes, 5% (Gertner, 1978). The "blockbuster" movie will not be too concerned about the magnitude of these costs up to a certain point; in fact, the budgets for such movies escalated astronomically in the 1970s and 1980s. For example, the *French Connection* cost $2.4 million to produce in 1971, *The Towering Inferno* $15 million in 1975, *Star Trek, The Motion Picture* $42 million in 1979, and *Annie, The Cotton Club* and *Santa Claus* $50 million or more each in 1982, 1984 and 1985 respectively. Admittedly, earlier years had seen extremely high budgets (such as *Cleopatra* at $44 million in 1963), but this tended to be the exception rather than the rule. By the 1980s, however, budgets of $20 or $30 million had become rather unremarkable. Moreover, the *average* production cost for movies financed by the majors more than doubled in the 1980-87 period, as did the average cost of marketing them (MPAA, 1988). Although the average production cost figure would be somewhat lower when *all* movies released (including independents) were considered — about $11 million rather than the approximate $14 million for the majors alone in 1984 according to Cohn (1985) — the majors tended to set the standard which the independents had to meet in order to compete. As Edmunds and Strick (1977:82) have noted in that regard:

> a small budget will restrict the use of stars, certain scripts requiring expensive set constructions, many location moves, long time-consuming filming, et cetera, which may add greatly to costs of production, and this may restrict the movie-maker in his choice of themes and film format.

Despite these restrictions, there was an increase in the number of these "lesser" movies once television displaced the motion picture medium as society's major form of entertainment. Television's situation comedies, police shows, and other programming categories proceeded to fill the role once filled by Hollywood's "B-movies." As William Fadiman (1973) points out, in this new entertainment environment, what once was a habit is now an occasion. Moviegoers are more selective in their attendance patterns; they go to *a* movie rather than to *the* movies. While creating turmoil as the old studio system (which was based on mass production and lowest-common-denominator principles) died away and was replaced, such a change in orientation allowed movies to become more specialized. It allowed moviemakers to seek out and satisfy various taste cultures (Gans, 1974) which tended to have fairly specific movie interests. Almost anything was possible as long as potential investors could be convinced that sufficiently large audiences could be attracted at sufficiently low costs. At the one extreme, this resulted in the production of pornographic movies with very loose to nonexistent scripts, bad "acting," cheap sets or locations, and the like (all of which contributed to the overall vulgarity which the audience was possibly seeking); at the other, it resulted in the production of works by Bunuel, Fellini, Antonioni, and Bergman, whose character development, cinematic virtuosity, and insights into the human condition gave credence to McLuhan's (1966) claim that a medium (movies) which is displayed by another medium (television) becomes an art form. After the crisis of the late 1960s and early 1970s, however, the major producer-distributors reemerged as the dominant force in the movie industry. Given their interest in the international appeal of movies and their reliance on the expensive, blockbuster-type movie to achieve it, "the tendency toward concentration of the industry and homogenization of . . . product [was] reinforced" (Phillips, 1975:181). The smaller, more specialized movie became less of a force in the movie marketplace as a result — although it did make somewhat of a comeback in the 1980s.

Regardless of the scale of a movie, however, the list of financial sources upon which a producer may draw remains basically the same. There are several categories of potential investors, the exact combination varying from movie to movie. The five basic sources include individual private investment, bank loans and other forms of corporate financing, government investment and/or subsidy (domestic and foreign), co-production with foreign companies, and direct investment by a distributor or by an exhibitor (Drabinsky, 1976). Other possibilities include arranging to defer some of the production costs, such as laboratory and processing charges and, if it can be negotiated, part of the fees to some of the creative personnel (stars, director, and the like). These deferred payments obviously cannot constitute a terribly large proportion of the overall financing, but in some tight situations they can mean the difference between being able and unable to complete the movie.

In addition to variations in financing arrangements among individual movie projects within a society, different combinations of financial sources seem to gain favor in different countries. It was estimated in the early 1970s in the United States, for example, that approximately 90% of the total production dollar costs at risk were borne by the distributors (Howe, 1972). Other countries, such as Canada, the United Kingdom, France, Italy, and Israel, have recognized the need for government involvement to establish and/or maintain an indigenous movie industry. The governments of these countries have developed a series of financial subsidies and other "incentives" to supplement the forms of private investment available for movie production (Drabinsky, 1976). It has been pointed out, however, that such measures are often subverted by "runaway productions" of American subsidiaries which manage to qualify as indigenous productions and receive subsidy payments under these various schemes (Guback, 1974). Furthermore Guback (1985, 1987b) noted that, despite the American industry's free enterprise rhetoric, the Hollywood majors have been willing to accept — and in some instances have actively pursued — government financial assistance in the domestic market and "nonmarket" support in the international sphere.

THE HISTORICAL STRUGGLE FOR DOMINANCE

The international influence of the American movie industry and the important economic role of the distributors within it make these organizations a major force in the movie world. The dominance of these modern major producer-distributors is well established (Edmunds and Strick, 1977; Gordon, 1973; Guback, 1979; Larmett et al., 1978). The history of the movies as business and industry, in fact, can be conceptualized as a struggle for dominance among the various segments of the industry (production/distribution/exhibition). The earliest beginnings of the movies were marked by intense competition among entrepreneurs who functioned as their own producers and distributors and sold their products to nickelodeon operators. These original exhibitors would exchange programs with each other, but the brief length of these early movies necessitated frequent program changes. The exchanges (distributors) emerged to relieve the exhibitor of this troublesome activity (Stevens and Garcia, 1980).

The first push for dominance, however, came from the production level of the newly segmented industry. The Motion Picture Patents Company (MPPC) was a result of the horizontal integration of nine production companies and a film stock manufacturer. This trust attempted to tie distributors and exhibitors to exclusive contracts under the threat of withholding the product — and demanded $2 a week from exhibitors for this "privilege" (Stevens and Garcia, 1980). From 1908 to 1910 it managed to sign up 60% of American theatres (basically all of the larger ones) and later moved toward vertical integration, having decided that distributing their own product made more sense than relying on the exchanges. Many similar types of vertical and horizontal integrations occurred during this early period as the producers and the exhibitors jockeyed for advantage in controlling the flow of movies (Larmett et al., 1978).

Despite some minor setbacks, such as the dissolving of the MPPC and General Films Company in 1917 as a result of judicial decisions and innovations by independents, full vertical integration (production-distribution-exhibition) was established as the norm by 1930 (Larmett et al., 1978). This development led to the dominance of the studio approach: movies were produced in the most economical fashion on an assembly-line basis since the studio controlled all the necessary resources (stars, screenwriters, directors, technicians, and so on) and the audiences were large (making demand high). U.S. Justice Department antitrust actions were initiated in 1938, but it was not until 1948 that vertical integration was eliminated when the Supreme Court ordered the producers to divest themselves of exhibition activities. Strick (1978: 412) observes:

> The Paramount case opened distribution and exhibition channels to independent producers by prohibiting such practices as "block booking," collusion by distributors on clearance and run, zone arrangements . . . , discriminatory pricing arrangements, and fixing admission prices. It created a more competitive market in both production and exhibition.

These changes, however, came at a time of turmoil; the movies were losing a large proportion of their audience due to the introduction of television and other fundamental changes in society. The elimination of vertical integration, then, robbed the movies of the structural stability that had taken them through the Depression and World War II, and might have assisted them in dealing with their decreasing market share (Bernstein, 1957).

The 1950s were times of adjustment for the movie industry:

> This period saw the rise of independent producers, a search for new markets, rising prices, a new cost consciousness on the part of producers, the beginning of diversification in the major production companies, a trend towards the "block-buster" movie, and technological developments in screen and sound [Strick, 1978:413].

New markets were located in foreign countries, and production was shifted toward television's needs, so much so that by the early 1960s nearly three-quarters of Hollywood's work force was directly or indirectly employed in motion picture work for television (Balio, 1976). The movies appeared to have achieved a new equilibrium (despite some troubles in the early 1960s) until "the crisis of 1969-71" struck. During that period, six of the eight major producers experienced losses for at least one of the three years (Steinberg, 1978). These losses included $52.0 million for Warner Brothers in 1969 and

$77.4 million for Twentieth Century-Fox and $45.0 million for United Artists in 1970.

This problem resulted from the fact that the major producers were still thinking in terms of retrieving the audience lost to television by making very elaborate and expensive productions. In 1968, then, the majors had invested $1.2 billion in movies and projects for current release in a market that could support an investment in the area of $500 million. "The result of such huge overstocking was that the companies had to take gigantic losses as they wrote off the values of the films and television rights down to a realistic level" (Gordon, 1973:196). In light of these developments and the fact that "the production, financing and the distribution of films are irrevocably linked," the distributors have come to occupy the dominant position in the movie industry (Gordon, 1973:195). This ascendency of the distributors is due to three factors: (1) they know their business and part of this distribution knowledge can be transferred to the production-financing function; (2) distribution is so expensive and risky that they must have some control over the product they handle, and only they have the international sales outlets that allow enough theater access to generate an adequate return; and (3) only the distributors have the cash flow to be able to set off the losses against the successes, such risk-spreading being "more akin to merchant banking than it is to wholesaling" (Gordon, 1973:196).

MAJORS VERSUS INDEPENDENTS

Although agents may have taken on a certain prominence and the studios may have been weakened somewhat (Litwak, 1986), there is no doubt these major producer-distributors remained the dominant force in the movie industry in the 1970s and 1980s. Their share of the annual number of movies produced and distributed might wane and their portion of the theatrical film rentals might fluctuate, but over the long run their control of the industry would remain essentially unchallenged. The eight major producers (Columbia, Twentieth Century-Fox, MGM, United Artists, Universal, Warner Brothers and Disney) exerted this control through their seven distribution companies. (United Artists took over MGM distribution in 1973 and in 1981 MGM bought UA to form MGM/UA Communications Inc.) Between 1970 and 1987, their combined share of North American film rentals ranged from a low of 68% in 1971 to a high of 93% in 1982 (Murphy, 1988). From 1970-76 the average annual figure was 82%, for 1977-84 90% and for 1985-87 74%. Over the entire 18-year period, the eight majors averaged 84% of the total annual domestic rentals. The addition of figures for mini-majors Orion and Tri-Star (the latter which absorbed Columbia Pictures in 1987, the company becoming Columbia Pictures Entertainment) brought the average annual market share for these 10 firms in the 1985-87 period to 91%.

This concentration of market control has drawn the criticism of independent producers, exhibitors, and government researchers. In 1978, it also resulted in a series of both private and federal antitrust actions being instituted "against various segments of the industry for past practices, violations of the consent decree, price fixing, block booking and other anti-competitive activities" (Larmett et al., 1978:3). The problem would seem to be that the major producers-distributors had chosen to attempt to maximize the viewer/cost ratio by producing a smaller number of blockbusters (with higher production costs and larger audience requirements) rather than by producing a larger number of "lesser" movies (with lower production costs and smaller audience requirements). This approach had the effect of raising the costs of production beyond the means of most independent producers – or at least to a level that required the independents to seek the assistance of the majors at disadvantageous terms at some point during the production-distribution-exhibition cycle.

The evidence of these inflated costs was most obvious in the case of the salaries for stars and the rights for literary "properties" from which screenplays could be developed. It was quite common for a "big-name" star to receive several million dollars, plus a percentage of some portion of the box office gross for appearing in a movie. For example, in the late 1980s, Tom Hanks, Michael Douglas, Meryl Streep, and Paul Newman were in the $4-6 million per picture category, Jack Nicholson, Dustin Hoffman and Robert Redford were in the $6-8 one, Arnold Schwarzenegger and Eddie Murphy each received $8 million per picture, and Sylvester Stallone topped the field at $16-20 million (Knowlton, 1988).

This faith in star appeal persists despite Gallup's findings that suggest this "marquee value" of stars *follows* rather than precedes a box office hit and is not a good predictor of the popular success of a movie (Simonet, 1978a). It also defies the logic of a *Variety* study of the annual top 25 "grossers" between the late 1950s and the early 1970s, in which it was found that the percentage of such successful movies that "featured performers of *little or no evident boxoffice appeal* at the time of release" (italics added) rose from just 20% at the beginning of the period to over 50% at the end of it (Steinberg, 1978:402). Such post hoc statistical financial analyses are supported by audience surveys, which Austin (1989) reports indicate that the presence of stars is not an important factor in movie attendance decisions – although they might contribute greatly to the public's awareness and knowledge about a movie through publicity. Moreover, even the inclusion of the highest paid star, Sylvester Stallone of *Rocky* and *Rambo,* could not guarantee the success of a *Rhinestone,* a *Cobra* or an *Over the Top.* Perhaps it is the case, as Aljean Harmetz (1988b) contends, and Mark Litwak (1986) would seem to demonstrate for Stallone in *Rhinestone,* that a star can guarantee an audience only for movies in which the star's role and performance match the audience's expectations and image of him or her. Despite evidence of their lack of guaranteed success, however, the presence of a star or stars seems to add a semblance of certainty to the movie-making endeavor which it might not otherwise have.

In addition, the presence of a familiar name is a necessity to attract international investors and appeal to international audiences – the international market being an essential source of funding and income in the modern movie-making environment. In fact, foreign markets have always been important to the movie industry. Estimates of their contribution to total theatrical revenue vary and have changed over time, from 25-40% in the 1920s to a high of 53% in the early 1960s, down to 50% in 1980, then falling to 35% in the early 1980s and below 30% in the mid-1980s. By that point, however, the shrinking foreign theatrical market was being balanced by the foreign video and cable markets (Donahue, 1987). Nevertheless, the "international film," which Lees and Berkowitz (1981: 129-30) define as "a collection of stars and synthesis of stories that promise worldwide commercial appeal," continues to play a major role in the movie industry. In this regard, John M. Wilson (1979:13) has observed that "Non-North-American audiences still flock to see American movie stars, which means producers are scrambling and paying dearly for the biggest stars." As it stands, there are fewer than 20 such "name" stars in the United States around which blockbuster movies can be assembled and even fewer when foreign markets are considered.

The other area in which costs skyrocketed in the 1970s was the sum paid for the movie rights to books – the single most important source of ideas for movie productions. Increasingly larger lump-sum payments were being made, often in excess of $1 million. Literary agents were in their glory making lucrative deals for their author-clients.

When some of the more notable sales – such as Peter Benchley's *The Island* at $2.1 million, Carol Longmeyer's *Four Hundred!* at $1 million and Gay Talese's *Thy Neighbor's Wife* at $2.5 million – went cold at the box office or were not produced at all, the bottom fell out of the market (Friendly, 1986). Prices dropped dramatically and lump-sum payments ceased, to be replaced by two-stage or two-tiered deals. The first stage involved more modest sums (from $5,000 for a little-known author, to $250,000 for a big-name one) paid for an option on the book for a fixed period; if the option was not exercised it could be sold elsewhere. A decision to produce the movie, however, would necessitate payment of a more substantial price for the rights to use it (Haithman, 1986). For example, Alice Walker's *The Color Purple* was optioned for $100,000 and an additional $200,000 was paid for the rights when Steven Spielberg made the movie (Friendly, 1986). If certain big-name stars show interest in a particular book, however, studios can get in a bidding war for the movie rights in order to secure the services of the star along with the literary property (Friendly, 1986; Haithman, 1986). Despite the general depression of prices for such rights in the 1980s, a then vice-president of the William Morris talent agency has noted that there will always be "megadeals" when the right book is involved: exciting story, appropriate characters and an interested star (Friendly, 1986).

Although costs may have moderated somewhat in this particular area, we have seen above how overall production expenditures have risen sharply in the late 1970s and the 1980s. One component was the costs of various crew functions, which had also risen dramatically. The trend in this area drew the ire of the Italian Motion Picture Association. This organization claimed that U.S. producers had inflated Italian production costs by the salaries they were willing to pay, and the Washington Task Force saw this inflation of costs as a "device [which] has supplanted the previous practice of limiting a stars [sic] availability by maintaining them [sic] under contract" (Larmett et al., 1978: 10). Such production cost levels acted as a barrier to entry to the marketplace, ensuring that the major producer-distributors were the only enterprises that could operate with consistent success in such an environment.

In the late 1970s and early 1980s, however, there was a reduction in production by the studios (Donahue, 1987), combined with the growth of home video and an increase in the number of theater screens through multiplexing (Harmetz, 1988b). These factors led to the growth of independent production, and the picture shortage of the late 1970s became the "glut" of the mid- and late 1980s (see Figure 2.1). The period also saw the emergence and growth of several mini-majors: Orion, Cannon, Lorimar, De Laurentiis Entertainment Group, Tri-Star and New World Pictures. Labeled "boutique companies" by Harmetz (1988b), these operations lacked studio lots and the substantial film and television libraries of the majors (which can act to cushion the studios against bad results at the box office).

Despite notable commercial and critical success—Harmetz (1988b) observing that 40% of 1987 Academy Award nominations went to movies that were not made or distributed by the eight majors—things began to come unraveled for the independents and the mini-majors in the late 1980s. Since about 10 or fewer pictures generate roughly 60-70% of the business at all theaters at any given time (Mayer, 1983) and the majors generally have the bulk of such box office winners, most nonmajors are eventually relegated to the margins of the industry. As independent production increased through the mid-1980s, the majors stabilized their own output and increased their negative pick ups of independent production—i.e., movies that have been financed by nonstudio sources, for which the studios guarantee to pay a portion of the production costs and which they agree to distribute upon the delivery of the completed picture (Garey, 1983; Zimbert, 1983). A decreasing proportion of independently produced movies found any domestic theatrical distribution in the latter part of the decade, many going directly to video, and about 25% not receiving any domestic exposure (theatrical or video) at all (*Variety,* 1988a).

In light of these developments, a shakeout seemed imminent and appeared to set in during early 1988 when the majors started to recapture market share lost to the mini-majors in the mid-1980s. Several of the mini-majors were

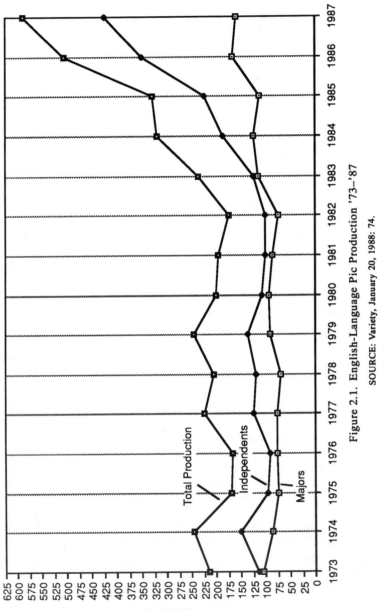

Figure 2.1. English-Language Pic Production '73–'87

SOURCE: Variety, January 20, 1988: 74.

faced with growing debts and declining income, and the majors were looking to buy up operations that still had something to offer. Orion appeared viable and Tri-Star had already merged with Columbia, but the other minis were vulnerable (Grover, 1988b).

PRODUCER-DISTRIBUTORS VERSUS EXHIBITORS

In addition to reducing competition at the production end, the high cost, small-number-of-pictures approach which the majors had adopted gave them an advantage in the exhibition area. Having been denied outright ownership of theaters by the U.S. Supreme Court's 1948 divestiture order, the major producer-distributors attempted to exert effective control over exhibition by virtue of their control of the flow of movies. The scarcity of product and the exhibitor's necessity to have movies in order to operate on a continuing basis meant that the producer-distributors had the upper hand in establishing rental agreements between the two parties. A product glut seemed to change this situation in the mid-1980s, although Guback (1987a) would contend that such a glut was more apparent than real: he noted that there did appear to be more pictures in this period than in the early 1980s, but the number was still substantially lower than that of the decade earlier. Nevertheless, the more important factor was that the majors continued to distribute the vast majority of profitable movies that the exhibitors were eager to have in their theaters.

Movie theater chains exercised considerable power in earlier times and "serve[d] as the cornerstone of Hollywood's monopoly power" (Gomery, 1979:38). By 1970 chains still controlled 53% of all movie theaters in the United States, and concern had been expressed about such concentration of ownership, as Sterling and Haight (1978) point out. The top six chains controlled about 12.5% of all theaters in the United States in 1975, and by 1987 a dozen companies controlled approximately 45% of North American screens with the four largest circuits operating almost 29% of them and having plans for further expansion (Yarrow, 1987b). The control of the total movie box office gross would probably be even more concentrated since the bigger circuits tend to own considerably more of the larger and more profitable theaters and fewer of the marginal ones. Although the chains' control of exhibition is not as extensive as the majors' control of the production-distribution segment, this concentration at both ends of the industry has lead Gomery (1983) to characterize it as a "bilateral oligopoly" — i.e., both areas being controlled by a small number of firms.

The three main practices that have resulted from the fact that distributors have the upper hand over the exhibitors are selective contract adjustments, blind bidding, and block booking (Larmett et al., 1978). In selective contract adjustments, preferential rates are given to cooperative exhibitors. Blind bidding requires that exhibitors enter into rental agreements for a movie sight unseen, often far in advance of its engagement. This practice limits the playing time for independent movies and gives the majors almost exclusive access to the most lucrative rental periods (Christmas, Easter and the summer). Blind bidding had been declared illegal in 24 states by the mid-1980s, at which time the main exhibitor and producer-distributor organizations agreed to a moratorium by the former of anti-blind bidding campaigns in additional states, and the cessation by the latter of efforts to rescind such existing laws (Guback, 1987a).

Block booking (also known as "tying arrangements") is the illegal practice of requiring exhibitors to rent a group or "block" of movies which includes mediocre as well as good ones, the mediocre ones being the price the exhibitor pays for the privilege of having the good films. Another practice that is gaining increasing attention is the "five o'clock look": this occurs when a distributor allows a preferred theater to inspect the other theaters' bids after the deadline so it can submit a bid high enough to guarantee securing the movie for screening. The distributors' advantage has also allowed them to impose "rough" financial terms on the exhibitors (see FINANCIAL TERMS below for specifics).

Exhibitors have responded to these tactics in a number of ways. One has been "skimming" or "siphoning," the underreporting to the distributors of the theater's gross receipts. Exhibitors have also been known to delay the remittance of rental payments to the distributors, prompt payment being especially important to the latter in days of high production costs and interest rates. Careful investment of these funds can earn notable investment income for the exhibitors (Guback, 1987a). Another more collusive activity has been product splitting, which is the perceived antidote to blind bidding and block booking. It is a practice which is normally limited to smaller markets, but has been banned by the U.S. Justice Department nonetheless. Vertical splitting (the more common form since it requires less communication among exhibitors) involves a division of producer-distributors and the assignment of each to an exhibitor whose bids are limited to that designated company; horizontal splitting, on the other hand, is done on a movie-by-movie basis.

A more fundamental approach has been the attempt to destroy the major's stranglehold on the marketplace by becoming involved in the production field to ensure a supply of product. Several attempts have been made at this approach, but none has enjoyed much success or been able to sustain itself. In the mid-1970s, members of the National Association of Theater Owners (NATO) were lobbied to pool their money to produce films through an entity labeled EXPRODICO (Exhibitors Production and Distribution Cooperative). Although the exhibitors agreed in principle, they seemed more inclined to pursue individual rather than joint ventures. A similar effort by the National Independent Theatre Exhibitors (NITE) a couple of years later attempted to raise collective funds for production investment through a national network of screen advertising. This avenue was thwarted by the majors' threats to withhold movies from those theaters agreeing to show ads (Donahue, 1987).

In the 1970s, then, the exhibitors blamed the reduction of movies being produced by the major producer-distributors for their problems. The majors countered this criticism, however, by blaming the exhibitors for creating their own misfortune by increasing the number of screens well beyond the production industry's ability to fill them. Dennis Giles' (1977) examination of the status of the exhibition segment of the movie industry in the mid-1970s would seem to suggest that both arguments contained a certain element of truth. There certainly was a reduction in the number of pictures produced during that period of time (see Figure 2.1). As for pictures released, Guback (1987a) uses the number of movies rated by the Classification and Rating Administration of the MPAA as an indicator of the number of movies available for exhibition in the United States. These figures demonstrate an almost 18% reduction of movies rated in 1977 as compared to 1975. The exhibitors were correct, then, about the availability of product. On the basis of data about theater screens (MPAA, 1979), the distributors would also seem to be correct, as the number of screens increased by over 10% in the 1974-77 period.

The discrepancy between the ways in which the producer-distributors and the exhibitors conceptualized this situation was largely attributable to the differences in their approach to the "risk-reward ratio." On the one hand, the producer-distributors chose to try to maximize their potential reward by minimizing the number of movies produced; on the other hand, the exhibitors attempted to minimize their risk (or make their returns more predictable) by increasing their exposure in the market (Giles, 1977).

In subsequent years, the number of theater screens continued to grow apace. By 1987 there were over two-thirds more screens in the U.S. than there had been in 1971, although the number of drive-in screens had declined while the number of indoor ones increased even more significantly. As Guback (1987a) has pointed out, however, the shrinking average theater size has meant that total seating capacity has not really expanded, and in fact was lower at that point than it had been in the early 1970s, and stood at just slightly more than half the level of the "golden years" of the late 1940s. The product shortage of the late 1970s and early 1980s has turned around, with the number of pictures released in 1987 reaching about what it had been in 1970 (Cohn, 1988). But a relatively small number of pictures continued to dominate the box office and to be the ones that the theater owners desired to play. Remarking that in the 1986 Christmas period the 10 most widely distributed movies were playing in close to 60% of all U.S. theaters, Guback (1987a:76) was moved to conclude that : "Clearly, the proliferation of screens has not necessarily meant a greater choice of films for consumers but merely more locations at which to view a small number of films."

Perhaps this change in conditions would account for the thawing of relations between the producer-distributors and exhibitors after the many struggles of the 1975-85 period (Guback, 1987a). And it might also account for the fact that the exhibitors did not seem to be overly alarmed by the majors

becoming exhibitors again — with NATO and the MPAA proposing the creation of an Exhibition-Distributor Council to foster better understanding
(Guback, 1987a). Despite the constraints of the consent decrees, the majors
had begun buying up theaters in 1985. The U.S. Justice Department's view
was that the confluence of the increase in theater screens and of independent
producers with the rise of pay-TV and home video meant such vertical
integration would not be a threat to overall competition in the movie business
(Yarrow, 1987a). By the end of 1987, distributors had acquired interests in
about 14% of domestic (U.S. and Canadian) theater screens, almost as high
as the approximately 17% of American theaters the five main defendants had
interests in at the time of the Paramount case.

THE RISE OF MULTIPLEXES

The increased exposure or risk-spreading noted above had been achieved
by the move toward "minitheaters" which seat only a few hundred people.
The other significant trend was the introduction of "multiplex houses" (or
"multiscreens") which are comprised of several minitheaters sharing a common main entrance, concession stand, set of washrooms, and projection booth
and projectionist (the latter perhaps not required at all if the operation is
automated). The sharing of facilities reduced overhead expenses, while the
smaller size counteracted the effects of product shortage since runs could be
longer (Barron, 1978b). These factors meant that a movie could gross as much
in a small house as it could in a larger one. There was also a great deal of
versatility in booking since adult-only and general-audience movies could be
booked into the same "plex," allowing parents to attend the former and their
children the latter. In addition, a movie could be moved from a larger to a
smaller theater once its appeal had waned, keeping that movie economically
viable and making way for a newer, more popular one (Drabinsky, 1976). In
1976, only 10% of U.S. indoor theaters were multiplex units (Gertner, 1978).
The increase in screens noted above, however, has come about through the
addition of such multiplex facilities — either as conversions of existing sin-
gle-screen locations or construction of new complexes. By the late 1980s,
then, the vast majority of theaters would be of the multiplex variety.

New multiplexes were built in places where people congregate to shop:
shopping centers, arcades, and malls. In addition, many older, larger theaters
(especially in city core areas) had been converted into multiscreens. Guback
(1987a) notes that such conversions were prevalent in the 1970s but that
construction of new complexes has been the dominant source of new screens
in the 1980s.

Typically these plexes have consisted of a small number of theaters of
modest but varying seating capacity (unlike "twins," whose two theaters share
facilities but are of equal seating capacity). In 1976, 80% of multiple screen
sites had two screens, while only 20% had from three to seven screens per

complex. Construction trends in the mid- to late 1980s indicated that economies of scale seemed to favor complexes of five or more screens (Guback, 1987a), with about 20 screens seeming to be an upward limit for such facilities. This trend has been accompanied by a decline in auditorium size in which average seating capacity dropped from 567 in 1972 to 342 in 1982 with even smaller facilities being reported built by some of the leading circuits in the mid-1980s (Guback, 1987a).

Stanley Durwood of American Multi-Cinema (AMC) would seem to be the "father" of the multiplex cinema concept. Introducing twin theaters in 1963, AMC opened the first four-theater complex in 1966 and the first six-theater one in 1969 (Durwood and Resnick, 1983). Initially concentrating on building such four- or six-theater facilities, the success of the multiplex concept encouraged AMC to change their expansion policy to include up to 12 screens in such developments. These moves made AMC one of the five largest U.S. exhibition circuits in the 1980s (Guback, 1987a). The company tended to concentrate expansion in those areas with future growth potential, namely the U.S. Sunbelt. They also "prefer[red] to locate theatres in middle-class areas inhabited by college-educated families and potentially college-educated young people." AMC considered these groups to be "the backbone of the existing motion picture audience and of our future audience" (Durwood and Resnick, 1983:329-330).

Spurred by the broader releases that distributors started giving movies in the 1970s, the multiscreen approach was intensified by the Canadian Cineplex operation headed by Garth Drabinsky. Cineplex introduced an 18-screen theater complex in the Toronto Eaton Centre in 1979, had plans for eventual expansion of such operations across Canada, opened a complex in Los Angeles in 1982, and by the early 1980s was doing business in 22 locations across North America. Buoyed by the purchase of the Odeon chain (Canada's second largest), Cineplex Odeon started its U.S. acquisitions in 1984 with the Plitt Circuit, eventually in 1988 becoming the largest North American theater chain. When Cineplex reopened refurbished movie houses in Manhattan that same year, and raised admission prices to $7, the company was the target of a highly publicized, but ultimately unsuccessful strike by moviegoers angered at the increasing cost of their favorite activity. Also criticized generally for the small screens and uncomfortable viewing situations of its earliest constructed auditoriums, Cineplex Odeon attempted to rectify the situation in later efforts with the development of comfortable and aesthetically pleasing "mini picture palaces," complete with original, locally-created murals in the lobbies. To add another dimension to the moviegoing experience, as well as potentially to increase revenues, Drabinsky experimented with selling lottery tickets in his box offices, introduced cafes licensed to sell beer and wine, and installed kiosks from which film-related T-shirts, souvenir books and soundtrack albums are sold.

DISTRIBUTION-EXHIBITION ARRANGEMENTS

While the introduction of multiplexes, and Cineplex Odeon especially, indicated changing exhibition procedures, the essential nature of the relationship between distributors and exhibitors has varied very little over the years, although specific terms may have varied somewhat (Beaupre, 1977; Mayer, 1974). Probably out of recognition of the unpredictability of the marketplace and the unique appeal and potential of each movie, however, there are several possible licensing arrangements that can be established between distributors and exhibitors. As the Canadian Motion Picture Distributors Association (1979:27) has observed: "No distributor has a uniform policy. The policy in each case is very much dependent on the picture."

Although the important producer may have some influence (and exhibitors may protest and suggest alternatives), the distributors are most instrumental in setting the "terms" for exhibition (Fellman and Durwood, 1972; Daly, 1980). These terms include the nature of the run, the date and length of the engagement, the type of advertising to be employed and the allocation of its cost between the distributor and the exhibitor, and the method of financial reimbursement for each party (Drabinsky, 1976; Fellman and Durwood, 1972; Hurst and Hale, 1975). The exact terms arrived at are governed by a number of factors: the determination of a "core audience" for the movie and its anticipated reaction to it, the availability of 35 mm prints (each of which is quite expensive to produce), the advertising budget available and marketing strategy to be employed, and the availability of theaters most suitable for the picture (Beaupre, 1977; Drabinsky, 1976).

RELEASE PATTERNS

The nature of the "run" (or the "release pattern" or "playoff") of a movie in a market is characterized by a combination of the *timing* of its release in a theater relative to its release in other theaters and the *number* of theaters in which the movie is being screened during the various phases of its run. The possibilities with regard to timing are first run, second and subsequent runs, and reissue or rerelease. First run is the initial screening of the movie, while second and subsequent runs occur in stages, each one starting after the preceding one has been completed. A reissue or rerelease, on the other hand, involves the reintroduction of a movie to the theaters after it has been completely withdrawn from the theatrical circuit for a period of time. Similarly, in the case of number of theaters, there is a threefold distinction. A run can be exclusive, in which case the movie is screened in only one theater; or it can be a multiple run in a large number of theaters; or it may be a limited multiple (or "red carpet theater") run which involves only a small number of theaters.

While the combination of the possibilities on these two dimensions would suggest a very large number of theoretically possible release patterns, in practice there is a more limited number of frequently employed practices. One such approach is the exclusive first run; that is, when the movie opens in only one theater in the market. After it has finished at that theater it may open in a second run in another theater in the market; this change is called a "move over." This process can continue for third and subsequent runs. An increasingly common approach is the first multiple run, in which the movie opens simultaneously in several theaters in the same market. The former is sometimes referred to as the *standard* release method and is employed for movies which are judged to have good potential, while the latter is known as the *showcase* method and is utilized to deal with high-budget, often star-studded movies of more questionable box office potential (Edmunds and Strick, 1977). The standard approach, then, attempts to maximize the effects of good "word-of-mouth" (that is, opinions delivered in face-to-face situations) which the gradual release should generate, while the showcase approach tries to reduce the impact of bad word-or-mouth. As shall be seen below, however, changes in approach have destroyed the standard pattern's claim to that title since initial broad releases are increasingly common.

There have been some additional variations of these two basic approaches. An exclusive first run might be followed by a limited multiple second run rather than an exclusive second run (Fellman and Durwood, 1972). In some instances, the movie might open in several theaters but only in the major markets, in a practice known as "day and date playing" (Canadian Motion Picture Distributors Association, 1979). Alternately, the movie might open as an exclusive, limited multiple run — which is also known as a "red carpet theater" run (Hurst and Hale, 1975). This is a method used to handle movies which are not considered strong enough for an exclusive first run but which are not felt to require a multiple first run. Another approach which has gained much attention since the success of *Jaws* is "TV saturation." In this approach, "more prints than usual are required and the picture is shown simultaneously in all or most of the expanded area covered by TV advertising which, for such pictures, is usually heavy. In each separate market in such areas, however, the picture still plays exclusive 'first run' or 'day and date'" (Canadian Motion Picture Distributors Association, 1979:31). Beyond the first run, there are numerous possibilities for the subsequent runs, in addition to the ones listed above. Beaupre (1977:49) describes them in some detail:

It may broaden into a multiple (or flagship) run; if that playoff maintains a high commercial profile, a subsequent *intermediate* run may intervene before the broadest possible saturation break. Or it may move directly from first-run to showcase, often supported in the latter dates by a second feature. At the end of the line is the so-called *underbelly* break.

One final method that has reappeared in certain isolated instances is a modification of the old "hard ticket roadshow attraction" which involves reserved seats for an exclusive first run and is designed to generate the idea that an exceptional motion picture is involved (Fellman and Durwood, 1972). The opening of *Apocalypse Now* in New York, Los Angeles, and Toronto, for example, was preceded by large newspaper advertisements containing order forms for tickets to this "reserved performance engagement" (which meant that "seating [was] guaranteed but not reserved"). This new variant of the roadshow approach is calculated to play on the advance publicity about the making of the movie and further adds to the impression that it is a significant cultural and social experience which should not be missed when it opens in other markets on an exclusive or multiple-run basis. Other examples, such as *Indiana Jones and the Temple of Doom,* would seem to have combined the sense of exclusivity of the reserved ticket for the roadshow attraction with the mass exposure of the saturation or multiple-run release. In all instances, however, the pacing of the playoff is a major consideration and involves the balancing of several factors, such as a sense of exclusivity, the availability of the movie to potential viewers, and the relative price of admission for the various runs (Beaupre, 1977).

A. D. Murphy (1983) notes that there used to be a three-tier playoff of movies: key first-run theaters; important neighborhood/regional and subsequent-run houses; and tail-end theaters or "dumps." Television dried up most of the last of these, and urban decay killed off many downtown key first-run locations, while suburban growth moved up many neighborhood/regional sites to first-run status. These developments reduced the pattern to a two-tiered one — first run and left over run — with Murphy suggesting that the latter was vulnerable to new technologies such as pay-TV and home video. A related analysis (albeit from a somewhat different angle) was provided by Peter S. Myers. Allowing that there could be variations of the dominant patterns he identified, Myers (1983:277) contended that:

> Basically, there are two release patterns for motion pictures: fast and slow. The fast pattern is for any well-known or easily exploitable subject that lends itself to a massive, national television advertising campaign. The slow pattern is for a more sensitive picture, without presold ingredients, which would require a gradual familiarizing of the public through favorable reviews and articles and the deliberate spreading of word-of-mouth, the single most important element in selling pictures . . .

The prevalence and importance of the "fast" method is underscored by Lawrence Cohn (1987) who noted that the number of movies which played nationally on 1,000+ screens remained at a constant rate from 1985-87 despite the drastic increase in production and releases during that period, with the majors maintaining a "rock-steady" pattern of such wide releases.

FINANCIAL TERMS

The financial arrangements arrived at between the distributor and the exhibitor for use of the movie is somewhat related to the nature of the movie's run, but the relationship between the two is not simple and direct. Traditional practice usually involved a "specified percentage" split of the gross box office receipts between the distributor and exhibitor, the percentage the exhibitor remitted to the distributor declining with each subsequent week the movie was played until some minimum percentage was reached (Beaupre, 1977). As an example, the exhibitor might have to remit 50% in the first week, 40% in the second and third weeks, 35% in the fourth week, and 30% thereafter. As an alternative to this "straight" or "fixed" percentage, the movie may be licensed on a "sliding or escalating scale" based on the level of box office grosses such that as box office receipts increase, the percentage that the exhibitor must pay the distributor increases as well (Beaupre, 1977; Drabinsky, 1976). Such an arrangement could specify, for example, that the exhibitor would remit 60% if a week's gross was $25,000 or more, 50% if $20,000-$24,999, 40% if $15,000-$19,999, and so on. In these gross percentage deals, the exhibitor pays his expenses out of the portion of the box office gross he retains.

A fairly common percentage split arrangement for first runs in major cities has been the 90-10 (over-house-expense) deal. In this scheme, the exhibitor first deducts the house allowance or "nut," which includes a profit margin (commonly referred to as "air") as well as operating expenses. He then remits 90% of the remainder of the box office gross to the distributor. In some instances distributors require guaranteed playing time; in others, guaranteed percentage minimums which decline with each week that the movie is shown (the latter usually being included in the 90-10 deals just described). These and other "rough terms" (large advances and detailed and minimum advertising campaigns) were usually only imposed (if at all) when the distributor had a "surefire" box office hit which the exhibitor wanted badly (Hurst and Hale, 1975). The distributor had to remember, after all, that a minimum level of good will with exhibitors was required since he would not always have such attractive fare to offer the theater operators. There is some evidence to suggest, however, that distributors might have forgotten this fact starting back in the mid-1970s (Mayer, 1976). They began to utilize the 90-10 deal more frequently and on a broader basis from the onset of the "blockbuster era," for example (Beaupre, 1977). This trend has also seen the general introduction of a guaranteed percentage minimum (also called a "floor") which is "a specified percentage of total box-office gross below which the exhibitor cannot pay, regardless of the application of the 90/10 formula," and was designed "to ensure against minimal payments for disappointing releases" (Beaupre, 1977:50). Some other provisions have included minimum per capita requirements—a fixed amount the distributor is to receive for each adult and child—which could be considered an indirect form of price fixing, and a "holdover figure" or minimum box office gross at which the exhibitor will agree to play the movie beyond the originally contracted playing time (Fellman, 1983).

In addition to these various percentage deals, there is also a "flat fee" or "buy out" approach in which the exhibitor pays the distributor a certain agreed-upon sum and keeps all the box office receipts himself. This particular arrangement is relatively rare, being utilized only for "tail-end runs" (Mayer, 1974), or "on second-feature pictures . . . [in] theatres of minimal grossing potential" (Fellman and Durwood, 1972). Lazarus (1983) has estimated that 85% of distributor-exhibitor deals are percentage ones.

"Four-walling," the exact opposite of the flat fee approach, was originally "a 1930s distribution method that had been used in the 1960s by low-budget filmmakers" (Donahue, 1987:225). It gained much broader interest in the early 1970s based on its successful use in the reissue of *Billy Jack* and in the release of several low-budget, independently produced wildlife and adventure documentaries such as *Alaskan Safari, Vanishing Wilderness,* and *The Ra Expeditions* (Beaupre, 1978; Mayer, 1974). In this form of deal, the distributor rents the theater and all the facilities for a specified period of time and keeps all the box office receipts from the screening of the movie. MGM's "Operation Blitz-Kreig" for the opening of *Westworld* utilized the heavy advertising approach that is characteristic of four-walling, but stopped short of complete imitation in retaining straight percentage agreements with exhibitors (Beaupre, 1978). While some of the majors adopted the four-wall deal outright for some movies and others followed MGM's more cautious approach for some of theirs, the "enchantment faded quickly" (Beaupre, 1978:72). A number of factors began to make the practice unattractive: the high risk connected with advance theater rentals impaired cash flow and profitability; many theaters began inflating their house nuts with "air," thereby pricing themselves out of the market; and in March 1974, the National Association of Theater Owners launched an antitrust suit that claimed the *major's* practice of four-walling constituted a violation of the 1948 consent degree (Beaupre, 1978). While the Justice Department did eventually rule in NATO's favor, the reasons for the demise of four-walling by the majors would seem to be more economic than legal. Beaupre (1978:72) succinctly summarizes the impact and the future of this practice:

> In the foreseeable future four-wall distribution is not likely to be employed by major companies with sufficient clout to guarantee collections from theaters. Its primary appeal as a playoff technique lies in its accelerating the rate of collections by small companies that might otherwise collapse under the weight of deferred receivables. However, the halcyon era of four-walling did awaken the industry to the value of television advertising and saturation breaks for major as well as exploitational releases. That education constitutes the legacy of four-wall distribution.

Donahue (1987:262) also notes that although the practice decreased in the 1980s it had a small but significant potential role to play: "Four-walling still remains a viable practice for a determined and dedicated filmmaker who wants to test his film or show himself and others that his picture can succeed with an audience."

ADVERTISING EXPENSES, CONCESSION REVENUE, AND SCREEN ADVERTISING

Another significant concern is the allocation of advertising expenses. In a percentage deal, this "cooperative advertising" is normally divided in the same ratio as are the box office receipts. Myers (1983) notes that Twentieth Century-Fox has also tried taking such expenses off the top of a theater's gross or asking exhibitors to commit a fixed amount. In the case of the 90-10 deal, the distributor may pay the full cost himself (Hurst and Hale, 1975). The distributor also absorbs the full cost of advertising in four-walling, while the exhibitor does so for the buy-out or flat fee arrangement. A first subrun (in which the movie is booked in a certain number of theaters in an area) is handled a little differently: each theater is asked to contribute a predetermined proportion of money over its regular advertising budget, and the distributor adds a certain proportion to this total (Fellman and Durwood, 1972). In all, it has been estimated that an average of 6 to 8% of a theater's gross is spent on advertising (Durwood and Resnick, 1983; Fellman and Durwood, 1972).

The manner in which that advertising money is spent (that is, how much money and in which media) is determined by agreement between the exhibitor and the distributor, although the exhibitor often makes decisions within a framework established by the distributor (Drabinsky, 1976; Hurst and Hale, 1975). The shift in emphasis to national advertising and promotion has reduced the exhibitor's role in such decision-making mainly to acquiescence (Mayer, 1977).

One facet of theater revenue that has been a bone of frequent contention is confection or concession sales — the proceeds from the sale of popcorn, candy, and soft drinks. By tradition, such proceeds have been considered the sole preserve of the exhibitor. According to Guback (1987a) patrons at indoor theaters spend $.35 on refreshments for every $1.00 spent on admission, and drive-in patrons spend even more. U.S. Department of Commerce data show that by the early 1980s, concessions accounted for almost 19% of total theater revenues. Given these figures and the fact that profits on such sales are approximately 60% (with some estimates ranging as high as 70%) while those on admission price are only about 1.5% (Larmett et al., 1978), it is little wonder that "some theaters have only been able to survive because of such revenue" (Drabinsky, 1976:162). (This situation is probably what led a Virginia Beach, Virginia theater owner to have a patron arrested when the man overlooked or ignored a sign warning against bringing in food, and refused to give up his two chocolate chip oatmeal cookies. When faced with a test of this policy in court, however, the theater dropped the charge and offered the offender and his wife one night's free admission.) It has also been claimed that the concession sale potential of a movie can influence the booking decisions of exhibitors (Donahue, 1987).

Four-walling did not materialize as a prevalent practice, a development which Mayer (1974) predicted would cause distributors to seek inroads even into this traditionally exclusive exhibitor revenue. Nevertheless, the distributor's argument for his share of this source of income has been made (Mayer, 1977), even if unsuccessfully to this point in time.

The distributors have been considerably more successful concerning another source of potential exhibitor revenue: screen advertising. Although enjoying a long and relatively strong tradition in Europe, the phenomenon has experienced only a very limited degree of success in the U.S. (Rotzoll, 1987). By the mid-1980's only a little over 20% of U.S. theaters were showing such screen ads (Guback, 1987a; Rotzoll, 1987). Distributors normally require that proceeds from such sources be included in the computation of theatrical revenues for the purpose of determining rentals due them and have generally been opposed to the utilization of such in-theater advertisements. A more important determining factor than distributor opposition in the exhibitors' failure to embrace screen advertising appears to be an attempt to maintain a sense of "good faith" with the audience by not subjecting this "captive" group to commercial messages in what has traditionally been (on the manifest level at least) a noncommercial environment (Rotzoll, 1987).

"LOOKS," "ADJUSTMENTS," AND THE ALLOCATION OF GROSSES

The distributor and the exhibitor enter into a formal contract for each and every movie a theater handles. While legally enforceable, most of these contracts in the past have usually been subject to "an understanding" that the parties to the contract can indulge in a practice known as a "look" (not to be confused with a "five o'clock look" which involves a distributor, in a blind bidding situation, informing a favored exhibitor of the highest bid after the bidding has ended, thereby enabling that exhibitor to submit a winning offer). This provision allowed them to "review and adjust" the financial terms in the exhibitor's favor, based on the movie's box office performance, before "the final settlement" was made (Canadian Motion Picture Distributors Association, 1979; Drabinsky, 1976: Fellman and Durwood, 1972; Mayer, 1974). This process was usually initiated by a dissatisfied exhibitor, either by means of a formal request or by simply reducing the original, agreed-upon amount when sending the distributor his share (Mayer, 1974). Distributors acquiesced in this practice for a number of largely legal reasons (Mayer, 1972). More fundamentally, however, this was another mechanism that was built into the system to cushion the effects of unpredictable audience behavior and maintain goodwill between distributor and exhibitor in the process. It should be noted that this renegotiation practice is not possible when the movie has been secured by the exhibitor in the competitive bidding process or when the contract explicitly states that such terms are nonnegotiable.

This old, established practice has been eliminated altogether in contracts for "important" movies (Mayer, 1977) as a result of the significant shift in power to the distributors. Numerous "rough" or strong terms have been implemented in such instances (Mayer, 1977): normally slow remittances from exhibitors to distributors are being expedited; auditing is being tightened up to prevent "underreporting"; termination of the license agreement by the distributor will be instituted for "failure to pay moneys in a timely manner, advertising contrary to agreed policy, insolvency, loss of control of the theatre, or breach of any other provision of the agreement on short notice" (Mayer, 1977:30); and payments of large cash guarantees and advances are demanded, the former being nonrefundable but the latter subject to renegotiation if the movie does not perform as expected. Beaupre (1977) suggested, however, that exhibitors would cease this "up front" financing of production once they have been "burned" by it.

Developments in the 1980s made such adjustments less common practice. Although distributor strength led to more frequent insistence on adherence to contract terms regardless of box office performance, the phenomenon had not disappeared completely. As Michael Mayer (1983:342) has noted:

This is not to say that the "look" or modification of terms after a play date is dead. For most minor distributors and an occasional major one, it remains a fact of life, contract or no contract. When an exhibitor cries that business was disappointing and he is losing his shirt, the distributor may adjust the terms of the deal regardless of the binding nature of the written contract. A distributor may feel deep sympathy or, more likely, a deep desire to license his next epic to the victimized theatre owner. But what was once the rule now has become the exception. The exhibition contract terms on film rental may no longer be characterized, as they once were by this author, as a "scrap of paper."

In looking at how the box office receipts are shared between distributor and exhibitor, Fellman and Durwood (1972) estimate that, on average, 35 to 40% of gross box office receipts is forwarded to the distributor, while the Canadian Motion Picture Distributors Association puts the Canadian figure at 33 to 34% (cited in Edmunds and Strick, 1977). These figures fluctuate over the years as the balance of power between the distributors and exhibitors changes: At the end of World War I the distributor's share of the box office gross was between 15 and 20%, and in the 1949-52 period it stood at 20-25% (Donahue, 1987); in the mid- and late 1950s it fluctuated between 30 and 40%; in the early 1960s it fell below 20% then rebounded to around 35% in the mid-1960s, but fell back to the 30% level in the early 1970s (Edgerton, 1983); it took off again in the late 1970s, reaching almost 45%, staying in that range until the mid-1980s when it again dropped below 40% (Donahue, 1987).

Hurst and Hale's (1975) "usable" but "incorrect ratios" have 60% of the box office receipts staying with the exhibitor, of which 20% pays the local advertising costs for the two parties and 40% pays the overhead and constitutes profit (but as the above discussion suggests, most of this 40% would go toward overhead). Of the 40% that is remitted to the distributor (which constitutes the "net film rental"), 10% is paid to the subdistributor; 10% pays for freight charges, national advertising, and the cost of prints; 10% is allocated to the producer—although Drabinsky (1976) suggests this may rise to 20%—and the remaining 10% is retained to pay overhead and constitute profit. If there is no subdistributor, the distributor retains that share as well, his total share then becoming 50% of the *net film rental* (Hurst and Hale, 1975).

THE DISTRIBUTOR-PRODUCER AGREEMENT

The nature of the agreement between distributor and producer also demonstrates the power which distributors wield in the movie industry. Since experienced and well-capitalized organizations are required to see that the product is made available and has access to markets, distributors can act as "gatekeepers" in the movie system, determining which movies can enter and on what terms. As Drabinsky (1976:145) observes: "If, but only if, a distributor . . . decides that the picture merits release and the kind of expenditures necessary to get it off the ground, the distributor will enter into a distribution agreement with the producer to govern their relationship." There are a number of provisions which such an agreement normally contains (Drabinsky, 1976). The first consideration is the *territory* that the agreement covers. While there can be worldwide rights, some producers (especially in "under-developed" movie countries such as Canada) may have to deal with several distributors: one for the domestic market (the United States and Canada) and several others for various configurations of the rest of the world. A second major term is *duration*. This period is normally in perpetuity if the distributor has contributed financial backing to the project. Otherwise it is 10 years if television rights have been granted, and as little as three years if neither of the above conditions pertain.

A third consideration which has become increasingly important in recent years is the *rights of exploitation*. These rights commonly deal with the way the movie can be marketed and publicized, the format in which it can be distributed (35 mm, 16 mm, video-cassettes), and the incredibly lucrative area "ancillary rights" for commercial "tie-ins" or "tie-ups"—products, services or commodities utilizing some aspect of the movie, such as soundtrack records, sweatshirts, lunch boxes, games, and toys. Furthermore, some distributors may request an outright grant of copyright, as well as remake, sequel, and television series rights — and now presumably "prequel" rights as well. In addition, they invariably insist on the right to alter the movie for the purpose of clearance by censors and sales to television.

Once all these matters have been decided, the distributor and producer must come to terms on the crucial issue of *manner of payment* of the producer's share — or, conversely, the method of determination of the distributor's fees and expenses to be deducted from his gross receipts (Drabinsky, 1976). The intricacies of the various procedures are an accountant's dream and are viewed by some producers as methods of unfairly reducing their share in the profits of the movies they have largely created. Intricacies aside, there are three main approaches to this manner of payback. In the case of a "lump sum buy-out of territorial rights," the distributor pays the producer a lump sum upon delivery of the components of the movie (picture and sound) from which technically acceptable prints can be made. The other two cases involve the distributor's fee being calculated as a percentage of the distributor's gross receipts. In the "net deal," the producer is paid *after* the distributor's percentage and various expenses (as decided by the distributor) have been deducted; in the "gross deal," he is paid *before* such fees are deducted. It is obvious, then, that the net deal will produce higher percentages (65-75%) than will the gross deal (25-50%), although the latter usually provides for the greater to receive a cash advance or guarantee and to start receiving his percentage earlier than he would in a net deal.

A variation on the gross deal, the "modified" or "adjusted" gross deal, involves the first dollar going for distribution expenses and the rest being split on an equal basis between the distributor and producer. Ed Colarik, a movie marketing consultant and independent distributor, claims that 40% of all movies are subject to gross deals (cited in Donahue, 1987). According to Barbara Boyle (1983:289) of New World Pictures: "Depending upon the negative cost of the picture, the higher the gross, the more favorable the adjusted gross deal is to the distributor. Conversely, the lower the gross, the more the net deal favors the producer . . . "

MARKETING IN THE MODERN CONTEXT

As Drabinsky (1975:9) observes, however, "Whatever the various deals that have been made, the question that still remains is whether people will be attracted to th[e] picture or not." A major determinant of how this question will be answered is the marketing approach or strategy that is adopted to attract the public's attention to the movie and to persuade them to attend it. While distributors "generally employ film promotors or marketing experts" to undertake this task (Edmunds and Strick, 1977:90), too often such decisions as the amount to be spent and the manner in which it is to be spent are based on intuition and past experiences rather than on thorough and accurate research.

By the late 1980s, $6-8 million was considered the *minimum* required to launch a major studio release and the *average* marketing costs per movie had risen to almost $9 million — there being a more than 100% increase in that average from 1980 to 1987 (MPAA, 1988). Moreover, it has been noted that in the 1970s the total of these expenses constituted approximately 15% of a distributor's *net rental receipts* (Edmunds and Strick, 1977), and in the 1980s represented about 25% of *total revenues,* a ratio that a (1983:270) described as "high for most industry categories in the United States, perhaps exceeded only by the cosmetics business." Given figures of this magnitude, then, the importance of correct decisions on these matters becomes readily apparent. Even more important than the sheer magnitude of the expenses incurred is the possibility that a properly planned and executed strategy can make a movie very successful. As an example, *Dirty Dancing* was produced for slightly less than $6 million and marketed for $10 million and was expected to produce $75 million in revenues for its production company, Vestron Inc. (King and Lieberman, 1988) — having surpassed the $50 million mark by the end of 1987 (Holden, 1987).

The types of "advertising" that can be used in the marketing campaign for a movie have been categorized by Morella, Epstein, and Clark in *Those Great Movie Ads* as paid advertising, publicity, exploitation, and promotion (cited in Hurst and Hale, 1975). (Kahn [1983] identifies the same basic categories but lumps the latter two together as promotion, noting that the term "exploitation" has gained a negative connotation that makes its utilization undesirable.) Paid advertising involves an expenditure to secure space in or time on one of the advertising media (newspapers, radio, television, magazines, billboards, and so on). Publicity is in effect "free advertising" since the media give coverage to some aspect of the movie because it is considered "newsworthy." Exploitation suggests a more conscious manipulation of the media since it involves obtaining publicity (and generating word-of-mouth) "by using gimmicks, stunts and other attention getting devices." Finally, promotion involves a tie-in between the movie and a product and/or personality.

A successful movie marketing campaign will normally employ all these approaches in varying degrees. There is a growing tendency to spend large sums of money on paid advertising. Donahue (1987) suggests that 50-60% of the negative cost of a picture is expended on all advertising, reporting also that distributors feel a campaign is successful when no more than 15% of the box office receipts has been so spent. Boyle (1983), however, suggests that both independents and majors spend an average of 30% of the pictures *expected* gross on cooperative advertising.

Expenditures on advertising are not spread evenly over the run of the picture; rather much expense if concentrated at the movie's opening. Charles Powell suggests that 80% of all advertising money is spent in the two-week period encompassing the week before, and the initial week of the movie's release (cited in Donahue, 1987). Donahue (1987:84) supplies an Orion executive's more detailed outline of the staging of a movie advertising campaign:

. . . the advertising costs for the pre-opening and the first week average $4.5 million. If the film shows any success and is situated in 800 to 1,200 theaters, $1.2 to $1.3 million is spent the second week. In the third week only $700,000 to $800,000 is spent. The advertising expenditures continue to decrease in the following weeks. However, in the seventh or eighth week, $1 million may be spent in the effort to renew interest in the picture. A blockbuster, however, may expend $20 million in marketing costs to sustain a long run.

The broadcast media have drawn increasingly significant attention and expenditures as advertising vehicles. This is especially true at the opening of a movie's run when 65% of its advertising budget is so expended (Ross, 1976). Such dependence on broadcast media (TV especially) has led to the move toward the TV saturation release pattern (discussed above), since it makes economic sense to allow a station's signal to determine the size of the market. Near the end of the movie's run, however, print advertising (mostly newspaper listings) accounts for almost all of its budget (Ross, 1976). According to Litwak (1986), newspapers remain a formidable advertising medium despite the increased prominence of television (due to the conceded superior selling power). In fact, 72% of the money spent annually on film advertising is expended on newspaper ads because they "must continue for the entire run of the film's release, while television ads typically appear for just two weeks to open a campaign" (Litwak, 1986:236).

While *The Godfather* broke the pattern of exclusive first-run releases, *Jaws* was the watershed for exhibition practices in that it "was the first major box office success to use the saturation booking technique along with massive national publicity" and "made promotion [in the broadest sense] the most important aspect of exhibition and distribution" (Daly, 1980). It opened in 464 theaters in Canada and the United States on June 20, 1975. In the preceding three-day period, a $700,000 TV advertising campaign was carried out as part of an overall advertising budget of almost $4 million. This campaign consisted of close to 75 exposures of pretested, 30-second spots in almost all prime-time programs on the three U.S. networks (Daly, 1980). When duplications are considered, 211 million homes were exposed to the commercials. Combined with newspaper and magazine ads, Universal had mounted a $1.8 million *preopening* campaign.

This strategy paid off handsomely. After only three days, the box office gross was $7,061,513; at $14 million for its first week, *Jaws* broke *The Godfather's* previous record of $10 million. Production costs were covered within the first two weeks of release and revenue continued to soar when 211 theaters were added in July and another 279 in August to bring the total to 954 theaters. By September 5, 1975, Universal announced that *Jaws* had surpassed *The Godfather* as all-time box office champion. This quick return established the pattern for top-grossing blockbusters, and almost every year seems to produce some new form of box office record in a business that has an array of statistics which appears to be surpassed only by that of major league baseball in its scope and intricacy: the three-day record was broken three years in a row in the late 1970s (*The Deep*, 1977 — $8.1 million; *Superman*, 1978 — $10.4 million; *Star Trek, The Motion Picture*, 1979 — $11.8 million); *Superman II* established a new three-day mark in 1981 with $14.1 million; 1982 saw *E.T.-The Extra Terrestrial* (the eventual all-time box office champion) knock *Superman II* out of the books for the highest *10-day gross* with $34.8 million; *Never Say Never Again* set an *all weekend* record of $11 million in 1983 (almost topped by *Crocodile Dundee's* $10.6 million in 1986); 1984 witnessed *Indiana Jones and the Temple of Doom* dethrone *Return of the Jedi* as the *six-day* champ with $42.3 million; 1985 saw *Rocky IV* set a *Thanksgiving weekend* record of $31.8 million; 1987 was the year Eddie Murphy's *Beverly Hills Cop II* set a *one-day* record of $9.7 million on the Saturday of the Memorial Day weekend; and the 1988 July 4 holiday was the occasion of a record $70 million *total* box office for a *four-day weekend*. All of these boxoffice records culminated in the last year of the decade when in the summer of 1989, the movie *Batman* took in $42.7 million the first weekend it was released. The crush to get into movie theaters across the country was so enthusiastic that it carried the entire boxoffice for all movies to more than $90 million for the three days. (Frustrated by unbearably long lines at some of its 2,194 screens, many people dashed to Disney's modest comedy, *Honey, I shrunk the Kids*, in large numbers, so that this film collected $14.2 million for the weekend.) After just ten days, *Batman* had earned more than $100 million. It was estimated that the movie might exceed the $400 million mark with ease in world-wide distribution. This boggling array of records reminds one of A.D. Murphy's (1983) caution that box office figures are often tools of "cheap puffery and aggrandizement" and of Aljean Harmetz's (1983a) observation that Hollywood gauges a movie to be a hit on the basis of a *per-theater average* rather than on overall gross — remembering also, of course, that *distributor rentals* are the figures used in calculating profit and loss.

To return to the issue of movie marketing in general and *Jaws* in particular, however, it should be noted that the "campaign" for the movie did not begin with the television "blitz" three days prior to its release. In fact, the selling of *Jaws* began in May 1973, two years before the movie's release and a year before the beginning of production, in a long, well-orchestrated campaign (Daly, 1980). The inception of the campaign consisted of a press release announcing the acquisition by Richard Zanuck and David Brown of the movie rights to Peter Benchley's bestseller and of casting plans for the movie. Universal kept releases flowing from that point, coinciding with growth in sales of the novel. Once production began, Universal transported hundreds of news people to the shooting location free of charge. It has been estimated that over 200 interviews were conducted with different individuals connected with the film, three times the normal number (Daly, 1980).

The release of the movie itself was planned to take place within six months of the publication of the paperback version of the novel and to coincide with the summer beach season. The cover of the book was coordinated with the advertising logo for the movie so that the two would create the "synergistic" relationship which would help each to sell the other. Zanuck and Brown sent out thousands of copies of the paperback to people who interact with many other people (such as cab drivers and headwaiters) and embarked on a Bantam-sponsored tour while Benchley was still on tour. This "pre-selling" of the movie in another medium is crucial if a movie is to become a box office hit since the public's advance interest in movies is minimal. In this regard, the Motion Picture Association of America has observed that prerelease publicity "seems unable to create extensive public awareness" for movies lacking "a tie-in with a familiar book or play or music" (cited in Daly, 1980).

The objective of such a marketing campaign for a movie, then, is to create an awareness of its existence among the potential moviegoing public and a desire to see it. In this regard, the Hollywood "rule of thumb" is that for a movie to generate successful box office revenues in its first week, 60% of that public must be aware of it and 20% eager to see it by the time it reaches the theaters (Harmetz, 1980). Furthermore, according to independent distributor Barbara Boyle (1983:290), "Anyone who understands the movie business will agree that grosses are achieved 70% by the film itself and 30% by marketing, sales, and promotion."

After the opening week, then, the picture is more heavily dependent on "word-of-mouth," and the subsequent marketing campaign and advertising expenditures are subject to the movie's own ability to generate revenue. A poor performance would likely result in reduced efforts and expenditures in order to cut losses, especially where the movie is released broadly with the attendant steep marketing costs. The desired result is for the movie to demonstrate "legs," i.e., the ability to keep the drop in box office gross from the opening to the second and subsequent weeks as small as possible — and more preferably to sustain or increase it. In the event of this latter scenario, increased marketing efforts and advertising expenditures are warranted given that one has the potential for a runaway hit. As Peter S. Myers (1983:281) notes with regard to the second weekend box office performance of a movie, if it "is as strong as the first, it's potentially a big-grossing picture; if it falls off by 20%, it can still be very big; if it falls off 40% or more, there's a real problem." An example of *lack* of such legs was Sylvester Stallone's *Cobra* (Windsor *Star*, 1986b). Released in 2,370 theaters during Memorial Day weekend of 1986, it took in $15.5 million the first weekend, falling 52% the second weekend to $7.5 million. By the beginning of July it remained on 1,115 screens but was grossing a paltry $1.2 million. With a total gross of only $48 million at that point, against a production cost of $30 million, *Cobra* was not to be the blockbuster success the presence of Stallone had seemed to suggest it would be.

The success of *Jaws'* marketing campaign, however, guaranteed a cycle of similar ones, just as a "breakthrough" picture spawns a series of imitations to cash in on the perceived audience appeal of its particular theme or plot line. One of the most thoroughly documented accounts of such a systematic orchestration of a marketing campaign was the "selling of *The Deep*" (Oddie, 1977). Based on another best-selling novel by the author of *Jaws, The Deep's* marketing efforts refined and extended the "cross promotion" or "piggybacking" between book and movie. It also utilized even more extensive publicity and promotional efforts, with numerous on-location interviews, television featurettes, a "making-of" book and documentary, tours by the book's author, and use of a video clip and free *Deep*-related promotional items at theme-related trade shows. Paid advertising involved the normally high expenditures on newspapers and television, special care on a theatrical trailer, unusually heavy utilization of billboards, exploitation of unique sounds of the soundtrack via radio to appeal to the youth audience, and a series of five magazine ads to tap the different thematic appeals of the movie for the various subgroups within the potential audience. Similar efforts to extract as much revenue as possible from various reworkings of *Buck Rogers in the 25th Century* (an upgraded television series/feature film motivated by the success of the series *Battlestar Galactica,* which in turn had been inspired by *Star Wars*) caused Peter Boyer (1979:14) to remark that after all variations of the property had been completely exploited in all possible markets, "presumably, the film will be chopped up and sold as guitar picks."

Modern motion picture marketing has come a long way from the crude efforts at exploitation and publicity exercised by the studios in the 1920s and 1930s — although even those elements still have a role to play today. The people who sell movies to the public have attempted to harness the practice of scientific market research to their ends. As Olen J. Earnest (1985) demonstrates in detail for *Star Wars,* this systematic approach to marketing involves title, concept, print advertising, TV commercial and trailer tests at the prerelease stage, as well as nationwide tracking of aided and unaided awareness, and postrelease surveys of audience reactions to the movie and their experience of it. The results of these studies informed the manner in which the movie was released and "sold" to the public at the various stages in its life-span (including rereleases). As Richard Kahn (1983:271) points out, however, scientific marketing research is not, and should not be followed slavishly in the movie industry:

> Motion picture marketing is not a computer science and never will be. Trained judgments, intuitive leaps, good guesses, and common sense must remain the hallmarks of motion picture marketing; if we veer from these criteria we're going to be in a great deal of trouble.

MERCHANDISING AND TIE-INS

Another area which has been in greater evidence in the "mass media mix" related to the movies (discussed in Chapter 1) is merchandising and tie-ins, which, as Drabinsky (1976) points out, become relied on more heavily to generate attention for a movie. Although such elements have been used in conjunction with movies for decades, and Disney has been particularly successful for years in their exploitation, the general consensus is that the watershed in movie merchandising was *Star Wars* — for which related merchandise grossed more than $1 billion retail, more than the movie itself took in at the box office (Blum, 1983; Lees and Berkowitz, 1981; Litwak, 1986).

The terms "merchandising" and "tie-in" are often used interchangeably, but Lees and Berkowitz (1981:155) attempt to clarify the relationship:

> The studios tend to define merchandising as being any instance of an outside company using a film title, or an image from a film, on a product or as part of an advertising campaign. This latter case is called a tie-in, and as its name suggests, it is a partnership of two different companies in a unified advertising strategy.

Furthermore, movie merchandise can be either generic products, which can exist independent of a specific movie but have a movie-related element incorporated into them, such as posters or T-shirts — the two most generally lucrative items according to Blum (1983) — or movie-specific ones such as a *Jaws* rubber shark or an *E.T.* character doll. Other variations can include the premium market, where retailers purchase movie-related items which they advertise as giveaways in conjunction with the sale of their products; the sweepstakes deal, in which a company sponsors a draw for a prize related to the movie — such as a trip to where the action in the film took place — after having paid a flat fee to use the name and the artwork of the movie in the contest; and a single advertising arrangement, whereby a manufacturer pays a flat fee simply to use a picture's logo in its advertising (Blum, 1983). Lees and Berkowitz (1981:158) described one Disney-Pepsi deal involving such an up-front payment or "trade-out," as one in which "Pepsi made an initial payment to Disney and then guaranteed that a like amount would be spent in advertising. The contract then made stipulations about the size and quantity of the ads."

The primary motivation for producer-distributors to enter into merchandising and tie-in arrangements is the promotional value they have for their movies; the potential revenue such arrangements might bring in is a secondary consideration. Although a valuable form of promotion for their movies, it is almost a point of honor that the movie companies would not pay a manufacturer to merchandise a product — but some producers "have been known to give licenses away when their films did not look like commercial contenders" (Lees and Berkowitz, 1981:157). This lack-of-financial-compensation type of approach is fairly common in the commercial tie-in area: the use of copyrighted movie materials may be bartered for references to the movie in a company's ads for its products, or movie-related items are provided free to use as giveaways by retailers selling products closely identified with the producer-distributor's picture.

Normally, however, a company must pay for the rights to use materials related to a movie in their commercial operations, particularly if that activity involves the manufacture of a product to which the movie is to be allied. To secure a license to manufacture such a product, a contract typically must include front money, a royalty and a guarantee. Blum (1983:381) describes these elements in some detail:

> Front money is good faith money that can range anywhere from $2,500 to $500,000 depending on the deal. It is really an advance against the royalty. The royalty covers everything sold at the wholesale price and is based on 10% of net sales. *Net sales* refer to gross sales less quantity discounts and returns. If the company's also going to agree to a guarantee beyond the front money, they will sell more aggressively because a guarantee is non-refundable. . . . The guarantee is due one year after the contract is signed. However, there's no standard deal. Most toy manufacturers won't step up to a 10% royalty rate; they would settle for royalty between 5 and 7 1/2%. In that case, all planning and designing is done by the toy company, with approval of samples vesting in the licensor and producer.

Two other elements usually included are approvals and exclusivity. The former is often required to allow the moviemaker to maintain quality control, and would also entail vetting by an actor (and payment to him as well) if it involved his likeness; the latter is less automatic, although the provision is obviously preferred by manufacturers.

Such movie licensing deals have resulted in a broad range of movie-related items being produced. The prominence of posters and T-shirts has been noted above, and other common items have included soundtrack albums, drinking glasses, sheets and pillowcases, blankets, towels, tote bags, lunch boxes, hobby kits, games, costume jewelry, iron-on transfers, inflatable toys, sleepwear, sweaters, underwear, etc., etc. Book publishing rights have commonly been considered separate from merchandising rights, but since the late 1970s, the distinction would seem to have blurred. For example, the 1983 release of *Return of the Jedi* saw: Ballantine Books publish five *Jedi*-themed paperbacks and planning for three more; five *Jedi*-related books claiming the top spots on the New York *Times* best-sellers lists in June of that year; and the B. Dalton Bookseller chain (the U.S.'s largest) selling more copies of the paperback novelization of the movie in the first week of June than any book they had ever carried.

The licensing arrangements for what are considered to be the right movies are extensive: Lucasfilm licensed the rights to *Star Wars* to 35 companies;

Universal signed contracts with 50 companies for *E.T.;* and Carolco Pictures Inc. entered into licensing agreements with 50 companies for more than 75 products for *Rambo III.* Jedi Adventure Centres were set up in shopping plazas to sell movie-related merchandise, while Universal opened an entire *E.T.* Earth Centre store for that purpose at its studio complex. Both *Star Wars* and *E.T.* had fan clubs established. This flurry of activity witnessed some unusual tie-in products in addition to the more run-of-the-mill ones: Pepperidge Farm character cookies for *Return of the Jedi,* so popular they had to be rationed to stores; an *E.T.* finger, which apparently didn't sell too well; *E.T.* ice cream, actually vanilla dyed an "other worldly" green and speckled with bits of Reese's Pieces; and a $2,250 "special edition" Rambo knife. Perhaps the most intriguing potential tie-in, however, was one that was not licensed – a Rambo prophylactic, which probably could have generated good sales, given the worry about AIDS in the late 1980s.

Concern about potential lost revenue and protection of copyright makes movie companies diligent in their pursuit and prosecution of companies and individuals who use likenessess of their movie characters, titles, and logos illegally. Just a few months after *E.T.'s* release in 1982, MCA/Universal had sued more than 25 companies for copyright and trademark law violations in relation to the movie, and had more than 300 other cases under investigation. Although such actions are normally aimed at large scale violators (such as an importer who had brought in 500,000 illegitimate E.T. dolls and had arranged to import 2.5 million more), some are more questionable. For example, two young men fed up with the *E.T.*-hype advertised "I hate *E.T.*" sweatshirts in *Rolling Stone* magazine, and received 200 orders before Universal ordered them to stop – which they did, returning the $6 each customer had paid. Similarly, an English professor was warned to cease and desist from publishing his four-page pamphlet which compared the *E.T.* movie with the life of Christ and which bore a cover with a sketch of the character drawn by an 18-year-old student. Having sold 23 copies and given away several free, the professor was treated in the same manner as the million dollar violators. Perhaps the fact that "a copyright that is not firmly enforced by its holder can sometimes be terminated by the courts" (Lees and Berkowitz, 1983:158) makes such rigid surveillance somewhat more understandable.

Video piracy was a major concern when *E.T.* was released on home video in late 1988. After initial theatrical release in 1982 and rerelease in 1985, the video version was brought onto the market in late October of 1988. The 10.6 million advance orders MCA had received for it – 3 million more than it was able to supply initially (Windsor *Star,* 1988) – and the prospect of $200 million in revenues (Metcalf, 1988) led to a number of anti-piracy measures: a colored as opposed to black plastic case housing the tape; unremovable hologram stickers on the cassettes and boxes; and recording via macrovision whereby attempts to copy it would result in images with wavy lines similar to those in poorly-tracked video (Shaw, 1988). The price of the cassettes was relatively low ($24.95 U.S. and $29.95 Cdn.) and was made even more attractive by a $5 rebate offer from Pepsi-Cola. The joint MCA/Pepsi-Cola promotional campaign was budgeted at $25 million, bringing posters and displays to 60,000 retail outlets and involving new footage of E.T. in the TV commercials for the video (Metcalf, 1988). The monetary results for this version of the movie, plus theatrical revenues, was expected to bring its total gross earnings close to the $1 billion mark (Metcalf, 1988).

Not all producers need exercise such vigilance over their movies, however, since many are not deemed suitable for merchandising deals in the first place, and few achieve the phenomenal success that makes the efforts of copyright violators worthwhile. Litwak (1986) identifies "action/adventure and fantasy films" as having the greatest potential in this area, while Blum (1983) describes them as "heroic, family-oriented, or youth-oriented" pictures, particularly with well-known actors. Lees and Berkowitz (1981) emphasize the "colorful, often exaggerated characters" necessary to appeal to children. Children, of course, are the primary targets of merchandising because most of such products fall into the category of toys and novelties, and children tend to be more brand-oriented and less conscious of the cost-versus-quality considerations of comparison shopping (Lees and Berkowitz, 1981). Building on these factors, merchandisers emphasize the concept of collectability so that children always have another item in a series that they will want to buy. Moreover, merchandisers aim to create a high degree of specificity in the items so that the child cannot exercise his imagination as readily with the toy, will become bored quickly, and will soon be asking for another item in the series or group (Lees and Berkowitz, 1981).

Nevertheless, even with these elements, a merchandisers's success is not assured in a realm Lees and Berkowitz (1981) describe as "a risk within a risk." Often companies will hold off as long as possible in committing expenditures, perhaps even until release of the movie to gauge its success. This approach, of course, loses (or at least blunts) the effect of the massive advertising and publicity at the early stages of a movie's release, especially for a successful one. The dilemma is particularly acute for toy manufacturers who need about a year's lead time to start their endeavors to be ready for the movie's opening. The success of Star Wars, for example, caught Kenner off guard, with no toys available for the Christmas following the movie's summer release; the company was forced to sell nonrefundable certificates redeemable the following April. On the other hand, early commitment to a box office failure can be exceedingly costly. For example,

First Brands Corp. spent $4 million last year to promote its Glad Bags with *Million Dollar Mystery.* The movie closed in a week. LIN Toys Ltd. took an estimated $1 million write-down when it abandoned production of *Howard the Duck* toys following that film's box-office flop in 1986. [Grover, 1988a:47]

In light of this risk associated with movies, plus the fact that they take a longer time to achieve their total audience than television and are only widely available for six months, as opposed to the more continuing nature of TV series (Blum, 1983), merchandisers are generally more attracted to TV than to the movies. This contention was borne out by a three-year decline in movie merchandising deals in the mid-1980s, coinciding with a boom in children's syndicated TV shows. *The Licensing Letter* reported that sales of merchandise licensed from movies and stage shows fell from $3.5 billion in 1985 to $2.2 billion in 1987 (cited in Grover, 1988a). At that point, however, the drop in ratings for many of the children's TV shows, combined with the saturation of the market with TV-related products, caused merchandisers to look again at a movie as "a [potential] big event that will produce a product to break out of the pack," according to a toy industry executive (quoted in Grover, 1988a).

In addition to the promotional value and the potential financial returns of these product and advertising tie-ins, there are other factors that demonstrate their growing importance. One is the ability of the success of certain tie-ins to influence the thematic content of movies. It has been demonstrated, for example, that in some cases there has been more money to be made from the sale of a movie's soundtrack than from the movie itself. This fact was felt to account for the large number of musically themed movies that went into or were slated for production in the 1978-1979 period (Barron, 1978c). In addition, the growth in importance of these ancillary rights is demonstrated by the fact that relatively large companies doing fairly large-volume business have emerged to specialize in this area — although admittedly they operate in areas of mass culture in addition to the movies (Barron, 1978a). These companies were thought to have some impact on the content of movies, nonetheless, since merchandising representatives have been allowed to read advance movie treatments and have suggested script inserts of ideas to assist in the sale of movie-related items (Safran, 1978). Lees and Berkowitz (1981: 163) would dispute this sort of contention, however, noting "that the scripts are submitted only to see if the toy companies are interested in licenses; the filmmakers don't want any creative input from the toy makers."

THE OSCARS AS A SELLING TOOL

One area that analysts often have ignored in the realm of marketing is the competition for Oscar nominations and awards. Although such campaigns very often witness an increased incidence of interviews with principals connected to the movies in contention, this struggle is largely masked from public view because it tends to be concentrated in media and direct contacts with the members of the movie community who do the voting (Davis, 1979). There are approximately 4,000 members of the Academy of Motion Picture Arts and Sciences, and about three-quarters of them are located in the Los Angeles area. It is this group that is the main target of the promotional efforts of the Oscar hopefuls, and they are courted by lavish ads in *Daily Variety* and *The Hollywood Reporter,* special screenings (often with cocktail parties), gifts of soundtrack albums, expensive promotional materials sent to their homes — and, beginning in 1979, saturation screenings on cable television (Davis, 1979).

Susan Stark (1983) reports that a Hollywood publicist estimated the cost of a "serious" Oscar campaign at $100,000, while Lees and Berkowitz (1981:166) claim that "studios, producers, distributors, and even the talent themselves spend an amount that totals hundreds of thousands of dollars every year." By the mid-1980s, estimates of the total expenditures by all parties involved surpassed $3 million (Davis, 1983). In return, the competitors anticipate reaping substantial additional box office revenue — and stars increased compensation for their movie appearances — from the receipt of Oscar nominations and awards. Industry estimates have put the value of a best picture award in the range of $10-$30 million and that of a best actor or actress one at from $3-$8 million (cited in Dodds and Holbrook, 1988). Anecdotal reports indicate that such is often the case, with *Gandhi* apparently taking in $30 million after receiving the Academy Award — almost as much as it had grossed before that event — and the 1982 upset winner, *Chariots of Fire,* selling an estimated $40 million worth of tickets because of the Oscar. There is also scattered evidence that would indicate that the impact of these nominations is not as significant as some would claim. *The Right Stuff,* for example, received eight nominations in 1984, but an expanded release from 100 to 627 theaters, in anticipation of a good Oscar showing, generated only $1.6 million over the U.S. Presidents Day holiday weekend following the nomination announcements — less than a fifth of the gross for the box office leader during that period.

One of the few systematic, empirical investigations of this phenomenon has tended to confirm Hollywood's conventional wisdom on the subject. Extrapolating from their analysis of the box office performance of 500 movies drawn from the *Variety* Key City Boxoffice Sample for the 1975-84 period, Dodds and Holbrook (1988) calculated that nominations for best actor, actress and picture are worth about $6.5, $7.0 and $7.9 million respectively, while a best actor award adds about another $8.3 million and that for best picture adds $27.0 million — with the results for a best actress award not reaching statistical significance. Nevertheless, Austin's (1989) survey of the admittedly sparse movie audience research on this specific subject reveals that moviegoers attribute very low salience to either Oscar nominations or awards in their movie attendance decisions. Conceding that these honors are publicity-generating vehicles that may assist a movie at the box office, Austin notes that the Awards' short-term and seasonal nature probably accounts for their "momentary and transient" influence on moviegoing behavior.

From the perspective of the members of the industry, however, Academy Award recognition adds a little more certainty to a highly uncertain area, and for that reason the efforts and expense seem worthwhile. Moreover, since an industry insider has ventured that as much as one-third of the Oscar promotional expenses goes to pleasing star, director and producer egos (cited in Kasum, 1983), a large portion of this endeavor can be considered an investment in human relations in a business heavily dependent on the performance of often temperamental individuals. Taken to the opposite extreme, the Oscars can become the focus through which a producer-distributor brings a movie to the attention of the public and the potential movie audience.

The Deer Hunter's owners, for example, were so concerned about the public's reception of their movie that they planned its whole release pattern around the Academy Awards ceremony (Lees and Berkowitz, 1981). Their strategy would seem to have paid off when the movie won the best picture award and went on to become "solidly profitable" (Windsor Star, 1979b). The 1979 campaign was also notable in that it added an additional "wave" of advertising and publicity to the normal first and second ones, which take place during the nominations and before the final voting, respectively (Thomas, 1979). That year a "third wave" (or perhaps more properly, "pre-first wave") was introduced before the "short listing" of the potential nominees in the art direction, cinematography, film editing, music, and sound categories. By the mid-1980s, it was being observed that the Oscar race seemed to be starting earlier every year (Windsor Star, 1986a).

"HYPE" CAN BACKFIRE

Such "hype" is not always successful, of course. Excessive campaigns and big spending can offend people and turn them against a nominee. Classic examples of this phenomenon are Chill Wills' loss after a blatant campaign for best supporting actor for The Alamo in 1960, and Diana Ross' (Lady Sings the Blues) loss to Liza Minelli (Cabaret) in the best actress category in 1972, as a result of what many people felt to be a heavy campaign that worked against Ross (Davis, 1979).

This type of "boomerang effect" is also possible in advertising a movie to the general public, as the example of The Great Gatsby most heavily underscores (Daly, 1980). Through a series of miscalculations (partially linked to an underlying power struggle), the movie was blown up by its marketing to a scale that the movie itself could never achieve. As Daly (1980) explained it, Gatsby was an attempt to create a blockbuster by fiat when "such a simple story did not demand the expensive production it was given. The audience might then have been led to expect too much."

In the late 1980s, several other examples occurred. A motion picture version of the underground comic Howard the Duck was a much touted offering in 1986 from George Lucas (of Star Wars fame). It was a box office and critical disaster, earning back domestically only $10.2 million of its $34.5 estimated negative cost. Leonard, Part 6 (attempting to build on Bill Cosby's

TV success) suffered a similar fate in 1987. It disappeared quickly and quietly after earning only $3 million versus an estimated negative cost of $27 million. Dustin Hoffman and Warren Beatty couldn't save the 1987 *Ishtar* — whose negative press began rather early. It managed only $7.4 million in box office receipts toward covering an estimated $45 million (or possibly as high as $60 million) production cost. (The monumental failure of the last led to a derisive Hollywood joke. Question: What's *Ishtar* mean in English? Answer: *Howard the Duck*.)

This danger of overselling their product is acknowledged by the people who run the movie business. While pointing out that the industry lacks the rigorous study of attendance patterns and motivations for attendance that seem necessary, Daly (1980) acknowledges that there are "experimentally derived procedures" that serve as *modus operandi* of movie marketing and distribution. One such procedure involves matching the amount of and cost of marketing of the "potential" of the movie and "the basic value of the property" (Oddie, 1977). Daly (1980) points out other such "procedures" that were learned from the success of *Jaws* and the failure of *The Great Gatsby:* the movie is released during one of the choice periods (Christmas, Easter, summer); it is licensed to as many theaters in each market as can be arranged; it is subjected to a massive advertising campaign with heavy reliance on the media — and well orchestrated in terms of timing and targeting of appeal as demonstrated by *The Deep* (Oddie, 1977); the movie is tied to, and cross promoted with, a successful book or record, or both; and the merchandise which is associated with the movie via tie-ins should be in keeping with the fantasy character of such blockbusters, being "extravagant and fun rather than utilitarian," and not demanding too much of a commitment.

Above all, moviemakers pay homage to "word-of-mouth," the recommendations that individuals make to their friends and acquaintances in face-to-face situations. While producer-distributors would prefer to have good critical reviews than bad ones, even the latter will be accepted if the audience has good things to tell its peers about the movie. Such a discrepancy simply adds support to the moviemaker's contention that critics are cultural eunuchs who know nothing about the business — let alone the art — of making movies. This concern with word-of-mouth would seem justified on the basis of research by Burzyski and Bayer (1977). Negative comments, made by confederates of the researchers upon leaving a theater, were found to have an impact upon those waiting in line to enter. Some waiting patrons even returned to the ticket booth and requested refunds. Hollywood can be expected to pay continued attention to this form of interpersonal communication about movies, and to attempt to refine and increase its role in the promotion of their product. Massive advertising will more than likely remain a major feature of movie marketing, however, until the pattern, established by *Jaws* and refined by later movies, proves to be unsuccessful — or a new, more successful approach surfaces.

CONCENTRATION LIMITS CHOICE

The organization and operation of the movies, then, characterize it as an oligopolistic industry (Larmett et al., 1978; Strick, 1978). There are a few producer-distributors who create and control the supply of movies, due to the high costs of production and other "barriers to entry" and "predatory and exclusionary tactics and practices" (Larmett et al., 1978). By choosing to emphasize the high-cost blockbusters which must appeal to mass audiences and therefore must be given elaborate and expensive marketing campaigns as well, the major producer-distributors limit the movie themes and treatments that can find their way to the screen. This tendency is reinforced by the growing reliance on the foreign market, making universal (but decidedly American) themes the most desirable, and contributing to a homogenization of the movie medium (Phillips, 1975). Even the "smaller" domestic movies that manage to get made, and the foreign ones that secure distribution, have little chance to be successful. In a sort of self-fulfilling prophecy, these movies are not judged to be "potential hits" and so are not given as intensive a promotional campaign as might be possible, with the result that they "sometimes never find their audience" (Daly, 1980). While many survive in spite of this treatment, few prosper and, as a result, the range of choice in mainstream movie theaters is not as wide as it could be under different market conditions.

Some empirical work in the mid-1980s, although apparently contradictory, would seem to lend credence to this contention. In examining a sample of movies produced in the 1940-79 period for evidence of "recycled" films (i.e., remakes, sequels and series films), Thomas Simonet (1987) attempted to test the hypothesis that conglomerate ownership in the movie industry led to a decrease in originality and creativity in movie-making. His analysis indicated that the period *before* such ownership actually involved greater recycling than after it, largely as a result of the high incidence of B-grade, series pictures, whose function was absorbed by TV in the early 1950s. Despite his rejection of the stultifying effect of conglomerate ownership, one of Simonet's (1987: 161) observations deserves further consideration in light of another study:

> The 1970s did see a slight increase in the number and proportion of recycled-script films in comparison with the 1960s, but the figures remained far short of those of the 1940s and seem to be explained by a correlation with total production rather than ownership. It would appear that originality suffers more in periods of high volume of production than in an era of conglomerate control.

The other study alluded to is Joseph Dominick's (1987) analysis of the relationship between film economics and film content for the 1964-1983 period. Although interested in the incidence of recycled films as Simonet had been (defining them as sequels and reissues, however) Dominick was also concerned with the more general effects of market structure on the variety of categories of movies produced by the industry. Overall, Dominick discovered "a rather stable industry that has adjusted to both good and bad economic times," but one which exhibited differences in the variety of its productions during certain portions of the entire period under study. In the hard times of 1969-73, when profits were down and before production costs had begun to skyrocket, considerable content experimentation took place. Less diversity of content, along with growth in sequels and reissues, characterized the consolidation period of 1974-78, as a result of rental incomes and profits increasing, the blockbuster becoming more common, and production costs beginning their upward spiral. The final period (1979-83) was marked by extreme conservatism as skyrocketing costs and pressures on profits caused the majors to reduce risks by reducing general movie variety, imitating one another more closely, and further increasing sequels and reissues. Although conglomeration per se may not have reduced originality and diversity, it allowed the majors to perpetuate the oligopolistic nature of the movie industry, to which Dominick attributed the developments he identified (along with demand uncertainty or risk). Moreover, despite the caveat that in the mid-1980s it might be too soon to make definitive statements about the impact of the new technologies such as cable and home video, Dominick (1987:152) noted that: "the data suggested that the new markets have not prompted much in the way of experimentation and innovation . . . Hollywood seems to be providing more of the same."

THE CHANGING INDUSTRY LANDSCAPE

All in all, there were some fundamental developments in the motion picture industry between the mid-1970s and the late 1980s. As Thomas Guback (1987a:76) described it from the perspective of 1986, "The industry landscape already is appreciably different from what it was a decade ago. Further changes in structure and policy are in store before 1990." The complex developments that have occurred are difficult to describe, let alone sorting out the causal connections with anything approaching complete accuracy. Nevertheless, an attempt has been made in Figure 2.2 to isolate and connect graphically the nexus of factors that contributed to the alteration in "industry landscape" during this period.

The exhibition side of the business witnessed "a mix of contradictory trends," in which the number of theater screens increased substantially despite the fact that ticket demand only remained stable and actually represented "an ever-increasing number of lost sales" when measured against population growth (Guback, 1987a). Guback attributed this increase in screens to a number of factors, most of them extraneous to the industry: First, there was the growth in shopping center complexes, of which theater facilities were felt to be necessary components. Leasing rather than building such facilities meant low capital investment and fairly high return for exhibitors. Secondly, the increase was due in part to the desire of some circuits to hold or increase

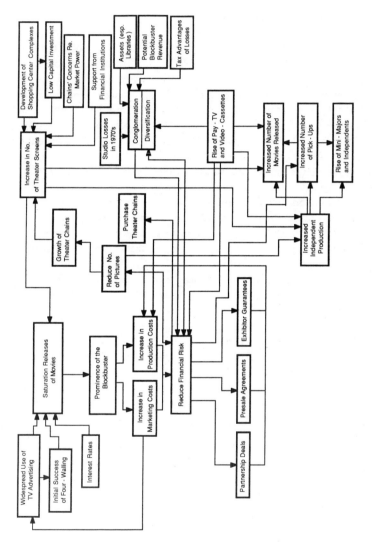

Figure 2.2. Factors Related to Developments in Motion Picture Production, Distribution, and Exhibition from the Mid-1970s to the Late 1980s

73

their market power over their competitors in the same area. Finally, this expansion (as well as the consolidation) of this segment of the industry was aided and abetted by "the active cooperation of the investment community . . .[which] not only has approved the current wave of construction and acquisitions, but . . . also has helped companies formulate and refine programs of consolidation" (Guback, 1987a:71).

On the distribution side, the emergence of the saturation release approach (in which a movie is made available to upwards of 1000 theaters at the same time) and its establishment as common practice was the most notable trend. As Cohn (1987) has pointed out, the number of movies receiving this wide-release treatment remained constant in the 1985-87 period (especially on the part of the majors), despite the drastic increase in movies produced and released in that time frame. Spurred by the initial successes of four-walling (that involved heavy utilization of TV advertising), the producer-distributors used this saturation release technique to take advantage of the broad exposure afforded by national TV buys. At the same time, the method accelerated the rate at which theatrical revenues were returned to them, reducing the interest paid on the money borrowed to finance a production — building on an established desire "to narrow the time window between the last day of shooting and the first day of release" (Lees and Berkowitz, 1981:75).

Such distribution practices reinforced the emphasis on blockbuster movies, which attempted to appeal to the widest and largest possible audience, and generate phenomenal box office returns and theatrical rentals in the process. The growing prominence and influence of this "blockbuster mentality" fostered the spiraling increases in production and marketing costs. With such large sums of money riding on individual pictures, the producer-distributors took steps to reduce or "lay off" their financial risks. Part of the solution involved securing outside financing through such devices as "partnership deals with investors, presale agreements with television networks and cable channels, and exhibitor guarantees" (Litwak, 1986:90). Ironically, the existence of this outside money actually contributed to the escalation of production costs since agents used it to demand increased compensation for their clients (A.D. Murphy cited in Litwak, 1986). Similarly, Simon (1987:1) has noted that the reduction of risk afforded by the new pay-TV and video-cassette markets was used "as justification for increasing total production costs rather than an opportunity to enhance profits substantially."

Other measures the producer-distributors took to alleviate their risk included reducing the number of movies produced internally. This move had the presumably unanticipated effect of reinforcing the tendency toward horizontal integration in the exhibition segment of the industry since the independents and smaller operators were unable to compete with the larger chains in securing this more lucrative product and were often "gobbled up" by the dominant circuits as a result (Donahue, 1987). Later, the majors moved to increase their output of releases by increasing the number of negative pick-up deals with mini-majors and independents, encouraging the growth of this facet of the industry in the process. (The initial emergence and growth of these nonmajors, of course, had been occasioned by the shortage of product brought about by the combination of the reduced number of studio-produced movies and the increased number of theater screens in the 1970s.)

In addition, the producer-distributors became involved in exhibition again, buying up substantial numbers of theater chains (as described in somewhat greater detail above). Guback (1987a:73) identified several reasons for this development, "although this is not to say that these reasons flow from an accurate assessment of the business climate." Direct ownership would allow (in their own theaters) control over ticket prices and other aspects of the retail end of the business, retention of all box office receipts (as opposed to sharing them with exhibitors), and an increased ability to determine theatrical release patterns — which would also have positive implications for the staging of releases in the post-theatrical markets. Other reasons included the ability to circumvent anti-blind bidding laws, and the simple fact that a distributor might fear a competitor would reap an advantage by having a presence in the exhibition realm and so purchased his own circuit or circuits to avoid that situation. Guback (1987a:74) noted, however, that there has been a considerable downside to such distributor involvement in theater ownership: "expansion into exhibition has entailed substantial commitments of equity and debt capital, balanced against the anticipation of future earnings."

Finally, major producer-distributors sought to diversify their holdings to cushion themselves against the vagaries of the motion picture marketplace. Conversely, conglomerates based in other areas of the economy began to view motion picture companies as potential acquisitions. Studio losses in the 1970s offered cash-rich corporations "opportunities to shelter income from profitable companies owned by the conglomerate" (Lees and Berkowitz, 1981:75). Furthermore, the studios possessed valuable assets, such as their movie libraries — which were typically undervalued on their balance sheets — making them attractive targets for takeover (Pryluck, 1986). In addition, movie companies offered the prospects of enormous revenues when their pictures were successful, and not bad tax advantages when they lost money (Lees and Berkowitz, 1981).

In the mid-1980s, these factors combined to produce a fairly buoyant situation in the motion picture industry. Toward the end of that decade, however, the shakeout cycle that should have occurred at the end of the 1970s began to take hold. The emergence and rapid growth of the pay-TV, then the videocassette market had deferred such an adjustment, but in 1987 Richard Simon (1987:4-5) observed that "For the first time in almost ten years, *there is no significant stimulative replacement technology on the horizon*" (original emphasis). Response to the shakeout began in early 1988, with the smaller producer-distributors who were facing growing debts and declining incomes becoming targets for "consolidation" by the majors (Grover, 1988b). Simon (1987:1) claimed, however, that *"for the better-run, broad-based companies it is a long-awaited culling process that is needed for the industry to enter a 'positive cycle'"* (original emphasis).

3

GIVING THE PEOPLE
WHAT THEY WANT
The Sociology of the Movies

The movies are an important social institution, going far beyond providing mere entertainment. They are part of the development of modern mass society, and they have helped to shape the way we live. Started at the turn of the century, movies were the ideal entertainment for the urban working class, but they also appealed to all classes in society. The movies were so popular, especially with children, that they sparked calls for social control and inspired many studies of "movie influences." The content of film can both "reflect" and "shape" society, and there is close identification with film stars. The audience for movies has always been a young one, and moviegoing is essentially a group activity. The movies continue to be a major factor in our popular culture today.

In 1917 the National Council of Public Morals in Great Britain issued a report on *The Cinema: Its Present Position and Future Possibilities* (National Council of Public Morals, 1917). The commissioners who presented this report stated their case for studying the movies in a forthright manner, and even today their comments are cogent and maintain their significance.

> [It] may be doubted if there is even yet sufficient realization of the strong and permanent grip which the picture palace has taken upon the people of this country. All other forms of recreation appeal only to a section of the community, but the lure of the pictures is universal. . . . [I]n the course of our inquiry we have been much impressed by the evidence brought before us that moving pictures are having a profound influence upon the mental and moral outlook of millions of our young people — an influence the more subtle in that it is subconsciously exercised — and we leave our labours with the deep conviction that no social problem of the day demands more earnest attention.

The initial purpose of the commission was to assess the motion picture's impact on the morals of the British people, but the implications went far beyond this objective. Even at this early date, the motion picture was clearly seen to be a new force in society, and, like similar commissions in the United States, this group was concerned with the speed with which this new form of entertainment had won public acceptance. The fact was that by 1917, the motion picture was the premier commercial entertainment form worldwide, and there was serious and very genuine concern about the supposed power of this medium to manipulate and influence audiences.

THE MOVIES AS AN INSTITUTION

It is necessary that we examine the emergence of the movies as an important modern institution against the social and cultural background which spawned it, for in many ways the movies were the first of the "modern" mass media, heralding the emergence of a true mass culture in the twentieth century.

Throughout the nineteenth century there had been numerous attempts to "capture the moving image" (Quigley, 1948; Ceram, 1955), and these culminated in the first important public showings of projected moving pictures at Koster and Bial's Music Hall in New York City on April 23, 1896. Exhibited at first as part of the bill of fare in vaudeville houses, where audiences were most enthusiastic over this new entertainment (Allen, 1980), by 1903 the motion picture had become a separately established entertainment institution, now being exhibited in specific locations, either rented halls or storefronts (known as nickelodeons), or later in theaters (movie "houses" or "palaces") especially constructed for the showing of movies.

There was a definite move away from being essentially a working-class entertainment toward a more middle-class activity, although the working classes continued their allegiance when the movies moved "uptown" (Jowett, 1976). The nature of movie content also changed as the industry made its middle-class aspirations obvious, and by the early 1920s, the major content forms had shifted from preoccupations with working-class or immigrant ideals toward a more sophisticated examination of the mythical world of some imaginary leisure class. As one movie historian has remarked of the people in these movies, they all had "lovely homes and lovely clothes and lovely cars and lovely lives. This was the desired, distorted mirror image of American 'normalcy' " (Baxter, 1968:35).

By the early 1920s the making and showing of motion pictures also constituted a major industry in the United States. By 1923 it was estimated that there were approximately 15,000 motion picture theaters in the United States, with a seating capacity in excess of seven and one-half million. The average weekly attendance at this time exceeded 50 million a week, and the box office admissions were close to $520 million. The total investment in the industry was calculated to be more than $1 billion (Wasko, 1982: 30-32). All in all, the movies were big business.

But the motion picture industry was more than just a successful business institution, for unlike steel mills or breakfast cereals the movies became an important factor in the actual shaping of the way in which Americans (and those in other parts of the world) thought and how they perceived the world around them. Perhaps more than any other social and cultural institution since the Catholic Church in the middle ages, the movies caught and held the imagination of hundreds of millions of people. The movies in many ways epitomized and paralleled the development of a "consumer society" in the twentieth century, and an eager public readily and enthusiastically embraced the "movie-star" as a symbol of both fantasy and success (May, 1980).

The motion picture was much more than merely entertainment or diversion from the humdrum routine of everyday living; there were other factors which helped to give the movies their prominent place in the American social structure. First, movies were the culmination of the development of a mass society in the United States, a process which brought together the dynamic forces of urbanization, industrialization, and the national forms of mass communication. When combined, these three forces created a form of social interaction which encouraged a greater degree of homogeneity in society than had previously been the case. Despite the diverse character of the American population, the increasing similarity of their socializing experiences meant that from a cultural perspective Americans were becoming more alike in their tastes. The mass media in general, and the movies in particular, were major contributors to this increased cultural homogeneity.

Second, the movies were the ideal entertainment activity for an increasingly urbanized population. Introduced with very little capital expenditure in storefront theaters in predominantly working-class neighborhoods, the movies soon spread throughout the city, often becoming the focal point for neighborhood activities (Merritt, 1973; Jowett, 1976). The movies were cheap—the entire family could attend for less than a dollar (which was important in an age when the average working man made less than $10 a week!); the movies were readily accessible, removing the cost of public transportation; and they were easy to understand because they did not require complete command of the English Language. (In later years title inserts were often translated out loud by patrons for those who could not read English.) These factors combined to make the movies the essential urban entertainment form, although, of course, it quickly spread to the rural areas as well.

In fact, the so-called nickelodeon age was relatively brief, and in the larger cities they began to disappear by 1908, when new exhibition practices were taking hold. Also, recent historical research has established that there was a substantial middle-class audience for the movies between 1906 and 1912, thus destroying the myth that the audience was entirely made up of immigrants or working-class people (Allen, 1982).

Third, the movies met with initial success precisely because this entertainment form was the logical extension and recombination of existing elements in the folk-popular culture continuum. Strong elements of the folk culture were to be found in the early content of these short movies shown in storefront nickelodeons, for as Alexander Walker (1970:61) has pointed out,

> It is worth emphasizing that the sentimentality of the plots, which jars today, was then very much a fact of life for nickelodeon audiences from the backstreets or immigrant ghettos where drunkenness bred brutish parents, long-lost off-spring were the common price of having to leave one's home-land, and the dying babies of melodrama had their statistical reality in the infant mortality rate.

Also, the creators of these movies were often from the same backgrounds as were their audiences, an important fact in folk culture where the relation-ship between creator and consumer is a close one. Later, as the movies became more sophisticated both in content and as an institutionalized form of busi-ness, the motion picture moved into the realm of popular culture, where the elements of folk culture were synthesized and refined into a product which had a more universal appeal. It is at this point that the movies begin to "shape" the ideas of their audience as much as "reflect" them.

The final factor which ensured that the motion picture would become an integral part of American life and culture was the adoption of this form of communication by a wide variety of established institutions, such as the church, schools, and government agencies. While these "noncommercial" uses of the medium were not as glamorous nor as widely appreciated as the entertainment movies, nevertheless, they were extensively used in a deliber-ately educational and communicative process, and therefore contributed to an overall acceptance of the motion picture as an undeniable fact in American society and as an integral part of the communication infrastructure.

Perhaps the greatest indication that the motion picture had become a recognized institution in our society was the furor surrounding the question of social control. No sooner were the movies exhibited publicly than attempts were made to censor them formally. These attempts culminated in the early period with a U.S. Supreme Court decision in 1915 (236 U.S. 230 [1915]). The court ruled that movies were not to be accorded the rights of free speech guaranteed under the First Amendment because they were not speech, and they were effectively relegated to the same entertainment category as carnival sideshows. The Court's decision stated in part:

> It cannot be put out of view that the exhibition of moving pictures is a business pure and simple, originated and conducted for profit, like other spectacles, not to be regarded, nor intended to be regarded as part of the press of the country or as organs of public opinion. They are mere representations of events and ideas and sentiments published or known; vivid, useful, and entertaining, no doubt, but . . . capable of evil, having power for it, the greater because of their attractiveness and manner of exhibition.

The constitutionality of this decision was open to question, and can only be understood in its historical context as part of the larger battle between the old guard Protestant group which had traditionally held political, economic and cultural control, and the new upstart immigrant groups (largely Catholic and Jewish) which were becoming more powerful. Very clearly the judges' decision was based upon the fear that the movies were potentially too powerful a means of communication to be left uncontrolled in the hands of often unscrupulous movie-makers (Jowett, 1986).

The result of this ruling was to give legality to the many types of formal prior-censorship bodies which would attempt to control the content of movies. These bodies or groups — be they at the state or city level, religious institutions, or even the industry's own self-regulatory agencies — were essentially aimed at one target: to make the movies more responsive to the audiences' needs and demands. (The issues of movie censorship are explored in greater depth in Carmen, 1966; De Grazia and Newman, 1982; Jowett, 1976; and Randall, 1968.)

THE MOVIES AS SOCIAL COMMUNICATION

As was noted in Chapter 1, the movies, as a form of mass communication, work essentially on the same model of communication as all other forms of mass media. However, some historical aspects of the manner in which the movies communicate are worth examining, for they help to explain why the movies, of all the major forms of mass communication in this country, were not protected under the First Amendment to the Constitution.

Figure 3.1 indicates one of the unique aspects of the movies' form of distribution. When first introduced, motion pictures were being made in several locations (New York, New Jersey, Chicago, Florida, California), but for a variety of reasons (such as climate, cost of land, and available scenery), the industry soon centralized in the Southern California town of Hollywood, near Los Angeles. It was here that the movie industry would create its product, to be sent out to the world. However, this centralized industry depended upon local exhibition sites as the point of contact between the "message" and the "receiver," and it was at this local level that the efforts toward making the movies more socially responsible were concentrated. The exhibitor essentially bore the brunt of the criticism, while he in turn tried to make the Hollywood industry aware of the problem. The questions being raised were related to the inability of the centralized source (the movie industry) to gauge the needs and values of the local community, and to create a product which would more accurately reflect these. (This is a constant problem made only more acute by the introduction of television.)

Figure 3.2 shows why this problem became such a major one. The movies (like the other forms of mass communication) are able to by-pass the traditional socializing agencies in our society such as the school, the church, and

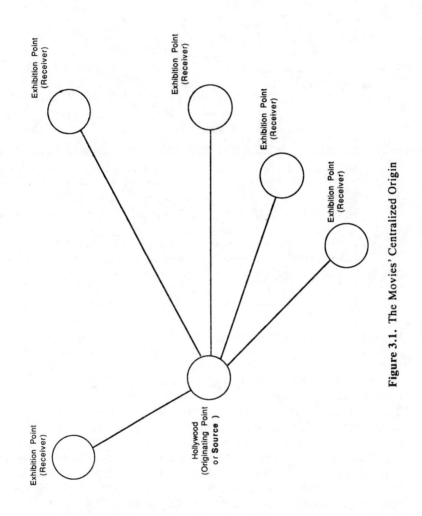

Figure 3.1. The Movies' Centralized Origin

Exhibition Point
(Receiver)

Exhibition Point
(Receiver)

Exhibition Point
(Receiver)

Exhibition Point
(Receiver)

Exhibition Point
(Receiver)

Hollywood
(Originating Point
or **Source**)

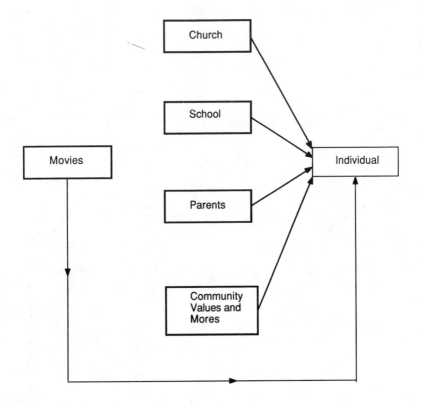

Figure 3.2. Model of Movie Socialization

parents and establish direct contact with the individual. Of course, we now know that whatever response is made to the "message" of the movies will be in accordance with the previous experiences of the individual, which takes into account the influence of these traditional social and cultural influences. But in the early part of the twentieth century, the prevalent psychological theories, combined with the relatively unsophisticated research methods then available, suggested that all human beings tended to act in similar fashion to the same stimuli. (The history of the development of our understanding of mass media influence is summarized in De Fleur and Ball-Rokeach, 1987.) Because the notion of "direct influence" on the audience was generally accepted, the movies were considered to be a powerful and influential source of ideas, and therefore to be as closely regulated as possible. (The actual nature of "movie influence" will be explored in the next chapter.) The important point here is that the motion picture was the first of the major mass media forms to attain this status of a "massive" socializing force on a national scale, and society simply did not know how to cope with it.

Thus, the movies as a social and cultural institution were the subject of numerous studies of varying scientific quality in a serious attempt to understand what effect they created and the nature of their role and influence in American society. In this early period far more attention was paid to the movies than to any of the other forms of mass media, mainly because of their high prestige in the world of popular culture and their obvious influence on such things as speech patterns, fashion, and other fads. This interest in the study of movies and specific research aimed at understanding the nature and extent of movies' effects declined almost completely after the introduction of television in the mid-1940s.

Ironically, television has actually increased the interest in movies by keeping alive the older movies and parading them over and over again for new generations of moviegoers. Thus, we have the example of a fifteen-year-old movie buff who has had the opportunity to see a movie like *Casablanca* far more times than the generation for which it was created. Unfortunately, this renewed interest in movies has taken the form of studies of movies, that is, in *examining* them, but not necessarily in paying attention to them as social and cultural influences.

THE MOVIES AS "REFLECTOR" OR "SHAPER"

The various forms of mass communication have all, at one time or another, been accused of "shaping" society. The question of whether or not the mass media are, in fact, capable of molding the minds of the audience is an extremely complex one, and the answer is subject to a wide variety of qualifications. "*Some* people are influenced by *some* media, at *some* time" is a commonly held belief by social scientists; but exactly how this influence takes place is still open to conjecture, as is witnessed by the continuing debate concerning children and television violence. (For a useful summary of research findings see Comstock et al., 1978. The history of the issues surrounding television and violence is discussed in detail in Rowland, 1983.)

It is more generally agreed that mass media are capable of "reflecting" society because they are forced by their commercial nature to provide a level of content which will guarantee the widest possible acceptance by the largest possible audience. Thus, there is a definite tendency to create a product which consists of familiar themes, clearly identifiable characters, and understandable resolutions. If the film strays too widely from these conventions, the audience will become confused and the result, especially for a movie made for entirely commercial purposes (as are most movies), will be a low return at the box office. The mass audience will simply not go to see a movie that it has heard is "difficult" or that deals with unpopular themes. Attracting an audience to a movie in sufficient numbers is a difficult enough process without having the additional burden of being considered intellectually challenging. It is for this reason that much of popular culture, and movies in particular, consists of the reweaving of old, familiar, comfortable plot elements.

The movies take as their starting point those aspects of society with which we have become familiar, but the license given to the creators allows plot twists and other narrative devices which infuse the story with sufficient new elements to attract an audience. The result is an interesting blend of the old and the novel; this is what John Cawelti has labeled "conventions" and "inventions" (Cawelti, 1969). The "inventions" which the movies' creators being to the familiar "conventions" provide the difference between success and failure. As an example, the success of a movie such as *E.T.*, which can be categorized simply as another "alien from a remote planet visits Earth" formula plot, is entirely due to the unique "inventional" contribution of the team assembled to make this big-budget ($30 million plus) production. Director Steven Spielberg was able to organize the combined talents of the writers, actors, set designers and, most notably, the special effects experts to produce a film which transcends the trite and obvious, and the audience responded accordingly by making it one of the most successful films ever produced. In fact, Spielberg has consistently indicated a unique ability to translate his own populist vision of childhood adventures into films which capture the imagination of audiences, while not necessarily finding favor with film critics. (These would include *Jaws, Raiders of the Lost Ark,* and *The Color Purple.*) The term "a Spielberg type film," referring to a plot which deliberately seeks to involve the audience emotionally in tension and/or deep emotion now has a specific genre meaning in the film industry.

The movies have always done a remarkable job in creating a type of visual public "consensus." While the relationship between the content of motion pictures and the role that such content plays in influencing the behavior of the audience is not easily understood, we do know that the movies were among the first of the mass media to create a new form of collectivity, the "mass public." As George Gerbner (1967) has pointed out: "Mass production and distribution of message systems transforms selected private perspectives into broad public perspectives, and brings mass publics into existence." The movies, as an entertainment medium, have been a potent "public message system" for more than 70 years. Thus, whether the movies are reflecting or shaping, they are contributing to the overall perspective we have of our society. Furthermore, they have made a significant contribution to the collective vision we all have of things about which we know very little.

Writing in the pretelevision period, Margaret Thorp (1939:19-20) pointed out

how rich the films are in facts and news, how much anyone can learn by going to the movies. . . . The small town boy in Vermont or Arkansas who has never in his life been fifty miles from the farm is now quite at home on the *Place de la Concorde,* Broadway at midnight, the Himalayas, or any one of a dozen South Sea islands.

The movies were powerful sources of "image-formation" in the twentieth century, and there have been many attempts to examine the movies as a source of imagery for the collective public consciousness, as well as playing a highly personal role in the psychological development of the individual viewer (Baldwin, 1976; Deming, 1969; and Rosenbaum, 1980). Recent film scholarship has consistently tried to find a connection between the images found in movies and the social and cultural tensions of the historical periods in which they were created (Biskind, 1983; Polan, 1986; Sayre, 1982). As Peter Biskind (1982:2) puts it:

> It has never been much of a secret . . . that movies influence manners, attitudes and behavior. In the fifties, they told us how to dress for a rumble or a board meeting, how far to go on the first date, what to think about Martians or, closer to home, Jews, blacks, and homosexuals. They taught girls whether they should have husbands or careers, boys whether to pursue work or pleasure. They told us what was right and what was wrong, what was good and what was bad; they defined our problems and suggested solutions.

THE MOVIE STAR AS SYMBOL

Much of the continued power of the movies as a social institution derives from the remarkably resilient status of movie stars in our entertainment firmament. The film star, male or female, is an enigma, almost a throwback to a past age, when "Hollywood" was a magnet to the aspiring youth of America (Rosten, 1941:12-16). Not very much has changed, and to be a "movie star" is still a position of considerable status in our society. While there are literally thousands of books which look at individual stars, surprisingly little has been written about the sociology of the star or celebrity phenomenon (Dyer, 1982; Morin, 1960; Powdermaker, 1950; Rosten, 1941; Schickel, 1985; and Walker, 1970 being exceptions) despite the importance it has in shaping our popular culture. We know a great deal about their lives, but very little about the essential nature of their appeal to the public.

One of the few sources for research on "star appeal" is Handel (1950), who summarized findings of studies undertaken for the movie studios. These studies were aimed at discovering not only the level of stars' popularity, but also the age group for which they had the greatest appeal, as this would allow the studios to mix younger stars on the rise with older, more established stars who might appeal to an older age group.

Clearly, one major element in movie star appeal is identification with the star. Despite what the old Hollywood moguls liked to believe, the majority of individuals prefer stars of their own sex. Handel (1950:145) cites one study

Table 3.1 Reasons for Preference of Stars of Own Sex

	Number of Mentions[1]
1. Conscious self-identification	35
2. Emotional affinity	27
3. Own sex better acting ability	22
4. Idealization, idolization	10
5. Admiration of fashion, styles	4

[1]Some respondents mentioned more than one reason.
SOURCE: Handel, 1950: 146.

undertaken by the Motion Picture Research Bureau in 1947, which showed that 65% of respondents asked to list their favorite movie stars showed a preference for stars of their own sex. This was even more apparent with men than with women; 76% of the men showed a preference for male stars, while 54% of the women showed an interest in female stars. When asked the reason for their preference, respondents' answers were classified as indicated in Table 3.1

In the neglected but interesting diary studies of both Blumer (1933) and Mayer (1948) there are many firsthand accounts of how strongly the identification with a movie star can be. One of Blumer's subjects noted:

When only fourteen year of age I fell in love with one of my classmates; I can remember that after seeing Rudolph Valentino in "The Sheik of Araby," I would try to make love to my girl as he did to the heroine, but I guess I was a miserable failure [Blumer, 1933:53].

This conscious attempt at imitation is echoed in other accounts, for once again, in the absence of competing role models, the movie and the movie star provide a powerful and convenient symbol for adolescents.

There has also been an interesting evolution in the type of star which attracts the public's attention. In the earliest period (1915-1931) movie stars represented a clearly polarized archetype. There were the "innocent" girls and the "vamps" (Lillian Gish and Theda Bara); and there were the masculine villains and the romantic, sometimes roguish heroes (Douglas Fairbanks, Sr., and Rudolph Valentino); but during this mainly silent era the characterization was of necessity quite simple. With the coincident arrival of both sound movies and the Depression, the movie star became a much more complex character—the good-bad personae emerged, to be eagerly taken up by the public, and stars such as James Cagney and Jean Harlow epitomized this new public adulation. The questioning of the underlying basis of American society during this period undoubtedly had much to do with the popularity of characterizations which clearly challenged authority.

For similar reasons, during the war years and immediately afterward the challenges outside America led to the reemergence of a more heroic masculine image (John Wayne) and a more servile female one (June Allyson), although by the mid-1950s the dominance of the youth culture, both as a fact in American culture and as a real factor at the box office, dictated the emergence of the "troubled, and misunderstood" youth rebel (James Dean and Marlon Brando). The female star during this period was required to project a blatant commercialized sexuality never before encountered in American popular culture (Marilyn Monroe, Jayne Mansfield, Elizabeth Taylor), and it was the female stars who most openly perpetuated the old Hollywood "star treatment."

By the early 1970s and all through the 1980s, the breakdown of the restrictive studio system and the resultant disappearance of the long-term contract led to the creation of the "strong-willed individual" actor such as Paul Newman, Marlon Brando, Steve McQueen, Al Pacino, Dustin Hoffman, Robert De Niro, and Robert Redford. These stars are more versatile than were their predecessors, playing a variety of roles (Brando being particularly adventurous in this respect) but with enough public identification to attract their own "fan" audiences. A phenomenon of the 1980s is the emergence of male actors who command such power at the box office that they are able to "package" their own film productions for studios eager to distribute the end product. Actors like Clint Eastwood, Robert Redford, and Sylvester Stallone (who made more than $10 million for starring in *Rambo*) seldom take on films unless they can produce or direct as part of the overall deal.

The major female stars also exhibit a strength of purpose associated with the new feminist ideals which emerged out of the late 1960s, and stars such as Jane Fonda, Barbra Streisand, Vanessa Redgrave, Meryl Streep, Debra Winger and Shirley MacLaine are outspoken individuals who would have had a great deal of difficulty surviving the rigidities required by the old studio system. (Bette Davis' experiences as a rebel in the studio system are part of the Hollywood legend.) However, for unaccountable reasons, few female film stars have acquired the same powers of control over their productions as the male stars mentioned above. (Barbra Streisand reportedly has such power, but a series of mediocre box office performances may have jeopardized this status.) What has changed is that the top female stars are often able to contribute to the development of the characters they are being asked to play, thus ensuring that the portrayal of women on the screen, long a subject of some concern for feminists, has become much stronger in the 1980s.

Whatever the characterization, the "star system" is a conscious attempt to manufacture an image which will correspond to certain public needs at specific points in time. The social and cultural tensions dictate the nature of the star, but it is (or was) the studio system and all of its publicity apparatus which deliberately created and promoted the image of the star as a primary means of selling the studio's product. As Morin (1960:135-137) notes: "The star system is a specific institution of capitalism on a major scale. . . . The star is a total item of merchandise: there is not an inch of her body, not a shred of her soul, not a memory of her life that cannot be thrown on the market." The mass merchandising of the star was not always an accepted part of movie-making, and, in fact, it was precisely the discovery that "movie" stars could be mass marketed which proved to be a major turning point in the development of the movie industry.

The early movie producers quickly learned that the anonymous individuals (one would hardly call most of them actors) they were using in their short movies were attracting audiences in their own right, and certain pioneers like producer Carl Laemmle were not slow in taking advantage of this new form of public hero-worship (Jowett, 1976:54-56). As Rosten (1941:329) has pointed out, "Hollywood learned that pictures with stars make money, and those without stars do not — or do not make as much as they would if they featured popular personalities. . . . The star system was hailed as the foundation of movie prosperity." Today, the star system (or perhaps "star-cult" would be a better term) continues to be an important cornerstone in the production of movies, and no major production can be contemplated until a guaranteed successful box office personality has agreed to star in it. The financial structure of the movie industry demands that such assurances be given, although what little research exists indicates that stars are *not* the major indicator of success in a movie (Simonet, 1980). Nevertheless, it is the movie star who remains the most important public symbol of the prestige of the movies in the entertainment hierarchy.

The marketing of show business stars and all of the attendant paraphernalia has become a very lucrative industry, with a wide range of spinoffs. Thanks to the power of television to keep their images alive, and the wide availability of videocassettes, even dead stars such as Marilyn Monroe, James Dean and Humphrey Bogart continue to have wide appeal. The merchandising of Monroe, in particular, has continued unabated, even though she died in 1962, and her image is one of the most recognizable icons in modern popular culture. The recent success of the rock singer Madonna is due in no small part to her deliberate cultivation of the Marilyn Monroe persona instantly recognizable to an audience born long after the star's death.

In the past the public was able to differentiate the "pure" movie stars (Brando, Newman, Redford, Pacino, De Niro, Fonda, Streisand) from those who floated between television and the movies (Garner, Van Dyke, Mary Tyler Moore, Savalas), but since the mid-1980s such distinctions have begun to disappear. Now such venerable "pure" stars as Charlton Heston and Elizabeth Taylor appear in television series or daytime soap operas, and claim that this does not diminish their status in the eyes of their fans. It is still true, however, that many of the top movie stars still prefer to avoid overexposure on television because they fear a diminution of their box office appeal, limiting their appearances on the "free" medium to certain specific instances that may serve their personal interests, such as political causes or the promotion of their latest movies. There is very little research to indicate the validity of this perspective. On the contrary, there is now an indication of an increasing trend to move back and forth between television and the movies as the two forms of entertainment become less differentiated for a new generation of audiences consumed by the video revolution. Nevertheless, there is still the subtle notion that a sign of success for a television performer is "making it in the movies." The recent film successes of actor Michael J. Fox are based to a large extent on his popularity in the television series *Family Ties,* but his greatest prestige has come from his work in movies such as *Back to the Future* and *The Secret of My Success.* (It is interesting to note that many film and television stars see the live theater as their haven of legitimacy!)

THE MOVIE AUDIENCE

Who constitutes the movie audience? What do they "receive" in return for their attendance at a movie? How are movie audiences different from audiences for other types of mass communication? It is rather difficult to believe, but movie scholarship has tended to neglect the audience entirely, and until recently, with the appearance of Bruce Austin's comprehensive survey of information on film audiences (Austin, 1989) there has been very little literature which adequately deals with the subject. The lack of scholarship in this area merely reflects the industry's own practices. Simonet (1978b:72) notes that much of the blame for inadequate research lies with the studio heads, for "they have always seen research as a threat when they haven't actually held it in contempt. After all, it is 'intuition' and 'insight' that allows executives to command high salaries." Austin adds that "The film industry uses audience research to answer one question: How can people be attracted to see a particular film" (Austin, 1989:2). If we examine the history of movie audience research, it becomes clear that industry executives more often than not ignored those findings about audience taste preferences which threatened to undermine their own instincts, even in the face of box office losses (Jowett, 1985).

It was not until the early 1930s that the first valid information about the composition of movie audiences was made available, and this confirmed what social critics had long complained about — that approximately 40% of the audience was under the age of 21 (Dale, 1933). Despite all the changes which have taken place in the motion picture industry in the last 50 years, the demographic composition of the audience had remained surprisingly stable until the last decade. Since the early 1980s one trend has emerged which could have a significant influence on the future of both the content and marketing of movies. Between 1979 and 1987 the percentage of the total movie audience over the age of 30 has increased from 24 to 38%. This is more in line with shifts in the population as a whole, where 48% of the population is over 30.

Table 3.2 Admissions by Age Groups

Age	*Percentage of Total Yearly Admissions*					*Percentage of Resident Civilian Population as of 1/87*
	1987	*1986*	*1984*	*1979*	*1976*	
12-15	11	14	13	20	14	7
16-20	21	21	23	29	31	9
21-24	15	17	18	14	15	8
25-29	15	14	13	13	16	11
30-39	18	20	18	11	13	20
40-49	10	8	8	6	5	14
50-59	5	3	4	5	3	11
60 and over	5	3	3	2	3	20
	100	100	100	100	100	100
12-17	18	22	21	31	20	11
18 and over	82	78	79	69	80	89

SOURCE: MPAA, 1976; 1987

(The data from a series of surveys undertaken by the Motion Picture Association of America are indicated in Table 3.2.) The key question is how will the movie industry respond? Will this mean a decrease in the endless stream of "teenpics" and "slasher films" aimed primarily at a younger audience, and the increase in the exploration of more serious themes? There was some evidence of exactly such a trend in 1987–88, but the long-range implications of this demographic shift are not yet clear for an industry which historically has been slow to react.

There has also been a trend toward a higher level of education in the frequent moviegoing population (Tables 3.3 and 3.4). While the increasing cost of going to the movies is one factor, it can also be surmised that frequent moviegoing has become a much more elitist activity, as television absorbs the interest of those with lower education. In predicting the future trends in movie attendance, the key variable will be the as yet unknown effect of the wide availability of the VCR across all socio-economic groups. (These as yet indistinct trends are discussed in more detail in Chapter 6.)

How much influence does the audience have on the actual creation and content of a movie? Obviously, the commercial movie is made with the audience's preference in mind, but is there any reliable feedback mechanism? This is one reason (as discussed in Chapter 1) why the studios are anxious to obtain properties, such as novels and plays, which have proven themselves. However, this ploy does not always succeed, because movie producers often fail to understand the audience's different needs and expectations of each of the various entertainment media. Herbert Gans (1957:315-317) suggested that there is an "active, although indirect interaction between the audience and the

Table 3.3 Frequency of Attendance

	Total Public Age 12 & Over					Adult Public Age 18 & Over					Teenagers Age 12 to 17				
	1987	1986	1985	1984	1976	1987	1986	1985	1984	1976	1987	1986	1985	1984	1976
Frequent (at least once a month)	23%	21%	22%	23%	25%	22%	20%	21%	21%	21%	47%	46%	48%	51%	52%
Occasional (once in 2 to 6 months)	27	25	29	28	26	27	25	28	28	23	37	34	38	34	27
Infrequent (less than once in 6 months)	10	11	9	8	15	11	11	9	9	15	6	10	3	6	13
Never	38	43	39	39	36	40	44	41	41	41	8	8	9	5	7
Not Reported	1	0	1	2	*	1	*	1	1	*	2	2	2	4	*

*Less than ½%

NOTE: Frequent moviegoers constitute only 21% of the public age 12 and over, but continue to account for 83% of admissions.
SOURCE: MPAA, 1976; 1987

Table 3.4 Frequency of Attendance by Education (percentages)

	Less Than High School					High School Complete					At Least Some College				
	1987	1986	1985	1984	1976	1987	1986	1985	1984	1976	1987	1986	1985	1984	1976
Frequent	4%	11%	5%	9%	12%	20%	17%	21%	23%	25%	29%	31%	34%	33%	29%
Occasional	16	13	20	19	11	27	27	30	29	28	30	32	33	32	32
Infrequent	6	11	7	10	14	12	11	11	8	16	11	11	9	8	15
Never	73	65	66	61	64	40	45	37	39	32	29	26	24	25	24

SOURCE: MPAA, 1976; 1987

creators, and that both affect the makeup of the final product." The audience makes its wants known by its willingness to pay at the box office and by what it has accepted previously. Moviemakers try to produce a product good enough to attract customers, but they also continue to guess what the audience wants and what may please them.

Gans, however, goes further:

> Every creator is engaged to some extent in a process of communication between himself and an audience, that is, he is creating *something* for *somebody*. This somebody may be the creator himself, other people, or even a nonexistent stereotype, but it becomes an *image* of an audience which the creator develops as part of every creative process. For analytical purposes their *audience image* can be isolated from the creative process as a whole. . . .

> It must be emphasized that the creator not only anticipates his audience, but tries to create or attract one for his product. . . . The "great" movie-maker may be able to create a loyal audience precisely because he knows or feels something, perhaps within himself, that is shared by a large number of publics, but has not been sensed by other creators who are perhaps equally bold or adept in other aspects of movie-making.

Thus, the movie is largely shaped by reference to real or perceived audience needs or preferences, or even prevalent public attitudes. (A good example of movies created to appeal to perceived or anticipated public attitudes are the two Vietnam War films, *Platoon* and *Full Metal Jacket,* both of which assumed that the American public wanted to see "what the real war was like" twenty years after the fact. Each achieved a modicum of success at the box office and critical approval.) And despite the increasing use of sophisticated research techniques, moviemakers continue to experience difficulties in predicting which movies will succeed (witness the disastrous financial returns for *Heaven's Gate* and *Chorus Line,* even though the latter had been one of the most successful stage musicals of all time).

While there has been a trend in recent years to create movies which will appeal to teenage audiences, with a rash of "splatter" movies such as the *Friday the Thirteenth, Halloween* and *Nightmare on Elm Street* series, the major moviemakers still depend on the appeal to a mass audience in order to make a profit. The challenge for today's moviemaker seeking to produce a box office blockbuster is obvious — to make a movie which has sufficient appeal to all segments of the population, and therefore maximize the size of the potential audience.

THE MOVIEGOING EXPERIENCE

"Going to the movies" is a social activity which almost everyone in our society has participated in at one time or another. While the frequency of attendance may vary, very few people have never had the experience of seeing a movie as part of an audience inside a darkened movie theater. If one stops and considers the apparent advantages of television and videocassettes as a source of entertainment (such as not having to dress up or find a babysitter, or use gasoline, or pay the increasing admission prices and the outrageous prices at the concession stand) we must seriously wonder why the movies continue to attract audiences at all! Obviously there is still something unique and inherently appealing about "going to the movies," and this is clearly different from other mass media experiences.

First, the content of movies is deliberately positioned to be different from that of television. While every moviemaker today intends to see his or her movie on either cable or network television at some later date in order to maximize profits, the initial intent is to provide a package sufficiently differ-ent from normal television fare to entice the audience to pay for the privilege of seeing the original theatrical release. If one is willing to wait long enough, every commercial movie will eventually turn up on the box in the livingroom, but that can take a year or more, although videocassettes are now available only months after theatrical releases. Therefore, one major factor is the payment for immediate viewing privileges. (It is this potential to combine the convenience of staying at home with the social need for immediate viewing that spurs the promise of "pay-per-view" cable. Audiences can still watch the movie during the first week of release without having to go to a movie theater.) Early viewing allows the individual to interact with others when the question of "did you see this or that movie?" arises. It is a means of social integration which signals that the individual is not too deviant from the mainstream cultural activities for his or her reference group. To have seen the latest hit movie, particularly in the first weekend of release, is a minor form of prestige; but more importantly, it is an absolute guarantee of admittance to conversation with others. We even use scenes from films as analogies to real life situations, or use dialogue from movies as a common means of expression understood by all. "Go ahead, make my day" from Clint Eastwood's *Dirty Harry* is now widely used, even by President Ronald Reagan. The movies continue to play an important role as a social integrator. (An in-depth examination of the various motivational factors involved in moviegoing is found in Austin, 1989.)

The moviegoing experience is overwhelmingly a group activity. Unfortu-nately, there is little current research on the exact makeup of groups attending the movies, so we are forced to rely upon a 1957 MPAA study. There is reason to believe that these trends have remained relatively constant, even though

Table 3.5 Movies as a Group Activity, 1957 (percentages)

Questions asked of respondents: "The last time you went to the movies, did you go by yourself or with someone else?"

	Total Admissions	Regular Theater Admissions	Drive-In Theater Admissions
Survey week's audience	100	100	100
With someone else	87	81	98
Alone	13	19	2

If "With someone else": "How many people went altogether, including yourself?"

Percentage of admissions accounted for by groups of two or more persons	Total Admissions	Regular Theater Admissions	Drive-In Theater Admissions
	87	81	98
Two	42	47	34
Three	14	15	12
Four	17	10	29
Five or more	10	7	16
Don't recall	4	2	7

SOURCE: Opinion Research Corporation, 1957.

there has been a major drop in the number of people going to the movies since 1957.

In a recent study by Bruce Austin of nearly 500 college students, the main reasons for going to the movies centered around seven basic motives as indicated in Table 3.6. Each of these motivations was analyzed according to the frequency of attendance, with "frequent" being more than three times a month or greater; "occasional" being once or twice a month; "infrequent" once in two to six months or less.

As Austin notes, two of the seven motives indicate a desire for "information," both learning specific information, and learning about "self." Thus audiences do seek to learn about the world of ideas and things from movies, while also seeking "introspective information" which provides personal insights. There are other, more obvious motivations, such as "to forget and get away and to escape" and "to pass time." These imply that movies fill a void in the recreational needs of audiences, and also provide a means of removing oneself from the everyday world by immersion in the action on the screen. Some people go to the movies to relieve boredom ("to be entertained"), or feelings of loneliness (in reality to avoid being alone). Finally, the motivation "to impress or conform to others" relates to the previous discussion of the role of movies as social integrator. As Austin notes: "This motive implies that the actual movie is almost incidental to the social integration value of the behavior" (Austin, 1989:57).

Table 3.6 Mean Scores for Movie Motivations Among Three
Moviegoing Groups[a]

| | Frequency of moviegoing | | |
Motivations	Infrequent	Occasional	Frequent
To learn information	1.55	1.64	1.86
To forget and get away and to escape	1.60	1.86	1.97
To enjoy a pleasant activity	2.13	2.41	2.56
To pass time	1.57	1.71	1.68
To relieve loneliness	1.11	1.11	1.19
To impress or conform to others	.84	.88	.91
To learn about self	1.05	1.13	1.34

[a]Higher mean scores indicate greater agreement with the motivation.
SOURCE: Austin, 1989, p. 57.

In the late 1980s, the movies, despite the obvious inroads of television, continue to be a central focus of cultural activities for a significant proportion of the population. As we have previously noted, the movies generate popular culture "waves" which affect a large number of cultural industries, and they are still the most visible and prestigious of the current forms of mass communication. Since the late 1970s, there has been a stabilization of the movie audience, although there will never be a return to the halcyon days of the mid-1940s. In fact, there are more movie screens in operation in the United States now than in 1948, when the admissions were three times as great. By the end of 1988, it is estimated that there will be more than 23,000 commercial movie screens, mostly in multiscreen complexes. However, the total seating capacity for indoor theaters is about half of the 11.7 million reported in 1948 (Guback, 1987a:67). What is clear in this apparently contradictory set of data is that a good movie experienced in the atmosphere of a movie theater is still considered a solid entertainment investment for producers and audiences alike. How long this will be the case in the face of the new array of competing delivery systems is unclear.

The social institution of moviegoing is firmly established in our society, however, and the movies have played an important part as one of the factors contributing to the dramatic changes which have taken place in the last 80 years in the way we live and also in how we perceive the world around us. They have provided us not only with entertainment, but also with ideas; and it would be difficult to conceive of our society without them.

4

KEEPING THEM IN THE DARK
The Psychology of the Movies

There have been many modifications in the way we perceive the movies as affecting the individual. Starting from the "direct influence" theory, the way individuals interact with movie messages has been subjected to close scrutiny. We now know that individuals can learn from movies and that the psychology of movie-going is subject to a variety of factors such as the social context, the type of movie theater, and even the type of content. The viewing experience involves identification and a willingness to ignore technique to concentrate on the narrative. The movie industry makes use of the psychology of the moviegoer both to measure the effectiveness of certain movies and to create appeals for new product. Movies do play an important part in the collective consciousness (or unconsciousness) of our society.

One major reason that movies were the subject of such intense scrutiny during the first 50 years of their existence as an entertainment medium was that they represented a potent combination of forces which were thought to be capable of causing dramatic behavioral changes in individuals. The movies were *perceived* to be capable of causing audiences to react in the way the filmmaker intended, and thus they were adjudicated to be "dangerous" and in need of close supervision. (It is important to note that those groups which concern themselves with protecting society from danger act on *perceptions;* the reality is not really important, but what is thought to be reality is!)

This "direct influence" theory of movie effectiveness was prevalent until the mid-1940s (and there are still some vestiges of it today — witness the furor surrounding the release of the motion picture *The Year of the Dragon,* which featured a storyline involving Chinese gangsters in New York City, and which was condemned by the Chinese community because they feared that it would convey a false impression of Chinese-Americans). With increasingly sophisticated research techniques being applied to the entire study of mass communication "effects" (Klapper, 1960; DeFleur and Ball-Rokeach, 1987; McQuail, 1987) the direct-influence model has been superseded by a series of theoretical assumptions which have in common only their underlying agreement that the factors which are in operation in the mass communication process are complex and defy simplistic analysis. We are no longer able to make simple statements about the "effects" of any mass medium; instead, we are forced to take into account such variables as the socialization experience of the individual; the predispositions which the individual brings to the communicative act; the context of the message; and also the physical, emotional, and even geographical environment in which the message is being delivered. Combined with the other factors affecting the communication process, such as source credibility, two-sided arguments, and the like (Hovland et al., 1965), it becomes obvious that we are dealing with an extremely complex issue.

In recent years, the emergence to prominence of the "critical studies" approach to the study of mass communication has added several new dimensions to the analysis of "effects." McQuail (1984:59-64) has arbitrarily and conveniently divided such approaches into three categories, each of which can be traced back to the original assertion by Karl Marx that "the ideas of the ruling class are in every epoch the ruling ideas." There have been several variations in interpretation of this assertion, the most identifiable of which McQuail calls, *political-economic media theory;* *"Hegemony" theory;* and *the Frankfurt School* or "critical theory." As he notes, each of these approaches has a different emphasis, but they operate from the perspective that "the study of mass communication is the attempt to uncover and unravel the complex mechanisms by which the production, distribution and consumption of ideological content is managed" (McQuail, 1984:63). There is a fourth category, *the "social-cultural" approach,* which has emerged as a type of coalition of the other three, and "is marked by a more positive approach to the products of mass culture" (McQuail, 1984:63). These approaches to the study of media promise to provide a much richer understanding of how the media operate in our society, especially in the analysis of competing power structures and the significance of the historical context. (For a more detailed introduction to this complex field, readers are referred to Collins et al., 1986.)

The question of the movies' influence on the mind, particularly because they were such appealing public entertainments, was examined by early psychologists such as G. F. Buckle (1926) and Hugo Munsterberg ([1916] 1970). Munsterberg, in particular, developed a rather sophisticated approach which centered on his belief that photography had a close relationship to reality, and that viewing movies provided "real" experiences for the audience (Fredericksen, 1977). The culmination of interest in movie psychology in the early years was the publication of the 12 Payne Fund Studies (1933-1935), which examined in detail the influence of the movies on American society. Under the generic title of "Motion Pictures and Youth" these studies were undertaken by reputable scholars who employed a variety of social research techniques, many of which were specifically developed for this project. The results of this major investigation, which ranged from the attempts to directly measure effects of movies on conduct to the sleep patterns of moviegoers, were not as convincing as many of the medium's critics had hoped. Instead, in a series of reasoned arguments, the researchers were cautious in admitting any evidence of "strong effects" but sought to place the question of movie influence in a more rational context, which clearly took into account factors other than moviegoing as the influences on an individual's life.

Herbert Blumer, who wrote the most controversial of these studies, *Movies and Conduct* (1933:196) made his position clear:

> It is insufficient to regard motion pictures simply as a fantasy world by participating in which, an individual softens the ardor of his life and escapes its monotony and hardships, nor to justify their content and "unreality" on this basis. For to many the pictures are authentic portrayals of life, from which they drew patterns of behavior, stimulation to overt conduct, content for a vigorous life of imagination, and ideas of reality. They are not merely a device for surcease; they are a form of stimulation.

THE PSYCHOLOGY OF MOVIE-VIEWING

The movies emerged at the end of the nineteenth century, a period in which the development of photography had set the stage for a reconceptualization of the notion of "realism." The public's acceptance of photographic realism as a standard to judge other visual arts affected the very basis of the human visual experience, and was a direct influence on painting, the theater, and even journalism (see Schiller, 1977). It has been argued by historians of the theater (Vardac, 1949) that the movies fulfilled the mass audience's desires for "pictorial realism," while others, such as Fell (1974), see the movies as part of an emerging visual narrative form, much akin to contemporary developments in comic strips. There is no disagreement among all these historical theories that, whatever the reasons, the movies became immensely popular among the entire population in a very short period of time (1896-1905).

The reasons for this popularity are not hard to establish. Movies provide a vivid visual presentation in which the images are already fully established, easily identified (in most cases), and easily followed. While we still grapple with understanding the complete psychological significance of the movie-viewing experience, it does seem clear that movies are conducive to ready comprehension on an elementary level. (There are those who see the "meaning" of movies as a set of complex interactions, operating on a lower, sometimes subliminal level. These will be examined later in the chapter.)

The ease of comprehension helps the viewer to assume the role of the characters and to identify with them quickly and effectively. If the aesthetic contributions of the close-up and the dramatic form are added to the vividness of presentation, it is not difficult to explain why the movies are such an effective form of communication. Also, the avowed purpose of movie producers is to induce this absorption or identification on the part of the viewer; and the viewer's basic goal when he or she attends a movie is to have just such an experience.

To satisfy this "need" for the moviegoer, movies have traditionally depended on appeals to the primary emotions and sentiments. While this is inevitably true of all drama, these simplistic emotional appeals tend to become exaggerated in the movies. While some use is made of abstract forms and complicated and remote symbolism in commercial movie-making, this is usually kept to a minimum. Instead, there is exploitation of what is primary and universal in human beings. Thus, emotions, passions, and sentiments are overemphasized. It is precisely because motion pictures deal with a mass of individuals of widely varying educational and cultural backgrounds that they find a common responsiveness on this elementary level.

What exactly takes place when one views a film? The audience comes to the film with an explicit set of assumptions, and these may range from a high level of expectancy of potential enjoyment to anger at having been dragged away from the television set at home. These predispositions are significant, for they clearly color the perception of the movies' "message." A complete analysis of what role these varied predispositions can play is not possible here, so let us concentrate on those viewers who come to a movie with the avowed purpose of being entertained. This could mean that they have paid their entrance fee in order to laugh, cry, be frightened or angered or sexually aroused, or merely to be removed from their everyday lives. Thus, when the lights dim and the curtains part, their minds are particularly open to receive the "message" of the movie. This sets the stage for an unusually strong type of communication process, because the viewer is willing, even eager, to receive what the communicator has to offer.

The special characteristics of the film-viewing experience, especially its supposed similarity to prehypnotic or dreamlike states, have long been remarked upon (Munsterberg, [1916] 1970). Tudor (1969) suggests that the darkened theater, combined with the heightened intensity of the message stimuli (as indicated above), the increased sense of social isolation that it creates, and the relaxed posture of the movie viewer make the message more emotionally potent and the viewer more susceptible emotionally to such stimuli than is the case with television.

Movies are typically characterized by the predominance of the "story film," or the "traditional narrative." This has been true for most of the history of filmmaking in the United States. In their important book *The Classical Hollywood Cinema* (1985), David Bordwell, Janet Staiger and Kristin Thompson, after examining more than 100 films over the period 1917 to 1960, make the point that there is a distinctive "classical Hollywood style" which is discernible. The authors note (Bordwell et al., 1985:3):

We would find that the Hollywood cinema sees itself as bound by rules that set stringent limits on individual innovation; that telling a story is the basic formal concern, which makes the film studio resemble the monastery's *scriptorium,* the site of the transcription and transmission of countless narratives; that unity is a basic attribute of film form; that the Hollywood film purports to be "realistic" in both an Aristotelian sense (truth to the probable) and a naturalistic one (truth to historical fact); that the Hollywood film strives to conceal its artifice through techniques of continuity and "invisible" storytelling; that the film should be comprehensible and unambiguous; and that it possesses a fundamental emotional appeal that transcends class and nation. Reiterated tirelessly for at least seventy years, such precepts suggest that Hollywood practitioners recognized themselves as creating a distinct approach to film form and technique that we can justly label "classical."

While movies can, and do, encompass a wide variety of techniques, styles, and subject matters, the most popular movies follow a basic format of "stars" featured in a series of events strung together in a more or less chronological format, referred to as "the plot" (Metz, 1974:16-28). This narrative is aimed at attracting the attention of the audience and intimately involving them as the sequence of events unfolds. The plot usually moves through a series of actions which alternatively raise and lower the audience's emotions, with the loose ends of the narrative being tied together rather rapidly at the end. Thus, narrative movies almost always have a clear beginning, middle, and end, and in that order. ("Films" which have attempted variations on this linear sequence often have difficulties at the box office.)

The object of the moviemaker, then, becomes one of persuading the viewer to cross the distance that separates the viewer from the screen, and to enter imaginatively the space of the screen world to experience vicariously the events that occur within that world. This is where the emotional aspect of movie-viewing becomes important. The vicarious involvement affects the viewer both physiologically and emotionally.

For example, as the unidentified man carrying a knife stalks the unsuspecting woman through the jagged patterns of shadow and light in the deserted city streets, the viewer experiences fear for the fate of the endangered woman. This results in actual physiological changes; the heartrate increases, the palms may become sweaty, and the overall condition would be one approximating fear.

This intense vicarious involvement in the flow of events is brought about because of two principal factors. The first is displacement of attention, which allows the viewer consciously to ignore technique and style, while the narrative events become uppermost in his mind. The second is identification with stars, characters, story types, and situations.

The viewer's desire to "enter" the narrative events of the movie is matched by the moviemaker's desire to create a narrative which would encourage the viewer to do exactly that. This accounts for the attraction the narrative form has for the moviemaker, for, as Fell (1974:14) comments, the narrative form had originally "developed to guarantee unflagging interest by omitting the 'dead spots' of other drama, enlisting identifications with the performers and refining resources of suspense."

The technology of the movie also adds greatly to the masking of the techniques of narration. As Mulvey (1975:17) observes: "Camera technology (as exemplified by deep focus in particular) and camera movements (determined by the action of the protagonist), combined with invisible editing (demanded by realism) all tend to blur the limits of screen space." The entire movie is constructed in such a way to rivet attention on the story, allowing the viewer to become deeply involved with the characters in the movie and in the sequence of situations in which these characters find themselves.

This brings us to the second factor which involves the viewer in the intense movie-viewing experience — identification. The concept of identification has been invoked in various guises in film theory since its beginning (Dart, 1976). While there are few studies which attempt to measure empirically the nature of such identification, researchers generally agree that it exists. As Maccoby (1968:120) points out:

> The question of just what characteristics of a screen character will produce fullest identification among viewers is a fascinating and still largely unexplored issue. The ability to lead viewers into identification with the character is a major part of the screenwriter's skill, and so far belongs more to the sphere of art than science.

By "identification" we usually mean the "putting of oneself in the place of" or "empathizing with" one or more characters in the movie. It has been measured by "indications of emotional attachment or liking" (Clark, 1971), and the two principal forms that have been recognized are similarity and wishful identification (Feilitzen and Linné, 1975). In the former, the viewer identifies with those characters most like himself, while in the latter, identification occurs with those whom the viewer desires to be like.

It is in the identification process that the psychology of movie-viewing meets the star phenomenon, for, as Tudor (1974a) points out, it is the "central factor in the psychology of the movie audience." The identification with story type is apparently secondary, although some types of narrative meet certain deep-seated needs of their audience. This in turn leads to a more generalized preference for certain story types such as war films, westerns, musicals, or romance films, and individuals can build strong affinities with these. Movie viewers also identify with noncelebrity actors as a result of the actor's characterization of an individual immersed in specific situations. The audience's "point of view" is significant here, because it "is a mechanism whereby we experience contemporaneously with a character" (Branigan, 1975:64).

This leads us back to the audience's psychological makeup as a factor to be considered in gauging the "effect" of a movie. Movies are capable of acting as creators of ideas and attitudes, especially where viewers have gaps in their experience of these issues. The ability of the movies to transport an audience outside of its local cultural experience is a significant one and accounts for much of the concern about "movie influence." Thus, while movies may alienate people from their own local experiences, they also prepare people for a wider cross-section of society as a whole.

Blumer (1935:125) addressed himself to the problem of movie influence and pointed out that "motion pictures not only bring new objects to the attention of people but, what is probably more important, they make what has been remote and vague, immediate and clear." In this manner, the movies are most effective in creating and reinforcing stereotypes, for where initial familiarity is least, the depiction in a definitive and familiar way becomes the norm. It is for this reason that so much attention has been paid to movie content and influence, particularly by racial or ethnic minorities which have constantly been the victims of the stereotypes in "Hollywood versions."

MOVIE-VIEWING AS A COLLECTIVE EXPERIENCE

As we saw in the previous chapter, the experience of moviegoing is usually undertaken by more than one person. But even for the solitary moviegoer, the experience once inside the theater becomes essentially a collective one. In sociological terms the audience for movies is "an unstructured group" (Jarvie, 1970:89) in that it has "no social organization, no body of custom and tradition, no established set of rules or rituals, no organized group of sentiments, no structure of status roles, and no established leadership" (Blumer, 1951:186). Of course, as Jarvie (1970:89) notes, "any particular neighborhood audience, which in suburb or drive-in is likely to reflect some of the characteristics of the surrounding society it is recruited from, is less unstructured." The crucial point for Jarvie is that even here " 'the' audience . . . doesn't exist. Or, at least, it exists only in the minds of some sociologists of mass society."

The audience is a collectivity of heterogeneous individuals who have come together for the sole purpose of seeing a movie, and even here there is a wide variety of personal reasons behind the decision to attend. However, once the movie begins, the communicative interaction creates an audience from the heterogeneity, and a triadic relationship develops between screen and audience, as indicated in Figure 4.1. The message goes not only from the screen to the individual, but this message is interpreted, enhanced, amplified, diminished, or even misinterpreted by interaction with other members of the audience. This audience interaction is most clearly exemplified by the presence of one or two persons who laugh (sometimes too loudly) in the right places in a comedy, or perhaps in the wrong place in a drama. This sets the mood for the rest of the audience, who sometimes may object to the response if it is not in keeping with the overall mood intended by the moviemaker. A more pervasive type of audience interaction is the hushed, quiet concentration in a dramatic scene or the definite air of tension experienced in a horror film,

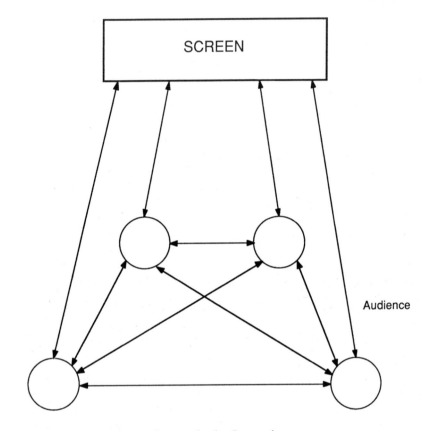

Figure 4.1 Movie Theater Communication Interaction

to be punctuated by screams of fear at appropriate moments. These collective moods contribute to the overall reception of the movie's message.

In exceptional circumstances, when the audience's emotions are deliberately being manipulated, such as in the series of *Rocky* films, or *The Color Purple,* the moviemaker has skillfully combined the various elements within the movie in order to elicit a "spontaneous" collective response. The spontaneity is carefully calculated, for as anyone attending these movies can see, the audiences always cheer in the same places, interact with applause as the hero wreaks vengeance after suffering a long period of tension-building humiliation, and the final denouement is always calculated to elicit a warm, self-satisfied response from audiences which obviously have a close identification with the major character and which see his victory as symbolic of the triumph of the little man over an increasingly complex, bureaucratic society. As an example, in the series of films featuring Clint Eastwood playing the

San Francisco homicide detective "Dirty Harry Callahan," there was a deliberate plot device which always ensures this desired audience response. Harry is continuously caught in the red tape of the police bureaucracy, which thwarts his attempts to deal with the criminals. Inevitably there is a turning point in these films, at which time Harry makes the decision to resort to a quasi-vigilante form of action outside of the normal police procedures. This is guaranteed to elicit a specific response, often accompanied by loud shouts of approval in the theater, as the audience prepares to see Harry defy authority and "really give as good as he gets!"

The drive-in movie offers another type of collective moviegoing experience. Here the audience of mainly adolescents is even more aware of coming together to form a new collectivity, and the rituals are carefully observed. Almost no one (except those actually interested in a movie they may have missed the first time around) actually goes to the drive-in alone. A 1982 study of the drive-in audience by Austin (1989:89-91) indicated that there has been a shift in the composition of drive-in audiences in the last three decades. The average number of individuals in a typical drive-in group is now 2.66 people, about one less than it was in similar studies conducted in the 1950s (See Handel, 1950). The 1950 studies had also found that the family group was the most prevalent unit, whereas Austin found that families only accounted for 16.7% of those in attendance. The most common unit was a male-female pairing, with males comprising 57.9% of the sample; the average age was 24 years, and 33% of the respondents were married. The atmosphere at the drive-in is very casual (children often come already dressed in their pajamas), but the major difference is in the alteration in the nature of audience interaction. Obviously, the audience does not interact by direct contact (although sometimes drivers honk their horns or flash their lights at particular parts of the movie). The interaction usually takes place within the smaller unit inside the automobile, and here too there are differences depending upon the size and composition of the unit. Four people interact differently from a couple; parents and children interact differently from parents by themselves. The actual viewing experience is typically more remote, lacking the intimacy of the movie theater; and the quality of sound, although closer, is usually poorer. And yet, the drive-in is an acceptable alternative form of movie experience; in fact, it is the only form of moviegoing for many in the population. (Of course, we should not fail to mention the relative seclusion of the drive-in as a place where adolescents and others may explore sexual activity with relative freedom. The drive-in has rightly acquired the reputation as a "passion pit.")

Thus, the psychology of moviegoing is dependent upon the type of viewing experience (large or small theater, drive-in, or airplane) and also the type of content. The content of the movie determines much of the expectancy of the audience, and while it might be too simplistic to say that audiences for comedies are happier than audiences for dramas, this type of behavior can be observed. In particular, audiences for films in the horror film/science fiction genre (the *Nightmare on Elm Street* series, *Aliens, Star Wars*) do seem to have a greater degree of expectant tension. All of this, of course, has been carefully fostered by the moviemakers. The promotional campaigns for such movies (*Nightmare on Elm Street* being an excellent example) almost always attempt to create the necessary expectancy in the potential customer by literally inviting the viewer to be frightened or to be otherwise vicariously thrilled.

THE USE OF PSYCHOLOGICAL TECHNIQUES IN MOVIE MARKETING

Increasingly, studios have been using sophisticated social science techniques to maximize their profit potential in movie investments. The making of movies has always been a business, first and foremost, and with the decline of the studios (as explained in Chapter 2) there is an increasing effort to market each film as a specific entertainment entity. During the last decade, there have been several examples of opportunistic marketing strategies which have worked for a while. In the late 1970s, one company, Sunn Classic Pictures, succeeded in developing a substantial audience for low-budget nature movies (*The Life and Times of Grizzly Adams, The Adventures of Frontier Fremont*), and pseudoscientific documentaries (*Beyond and Back, Chariots of the Gods, In Search of the Real Noah's Ark*) by using a sophisticated computer analysis to isolate the specific requirements of the potential audience for their product. As one journalist put it: "Every element of this heart-warming drama [*Grizzly Adams*], from the hair and eye coloring of the actors to the type of animals they frolic with, was pre-tested by a highly sophisticated computer technology. Your family's every 'ooh' and 'ahh' was anticipated in tests taken by other families demographically identical to yours" (Morrisroe, 1980).

Using test systems such as this, Sunn Classics achieved an enviable record of hits, and often used the marketing concept of "four walling" (see Chapter 2). The founder and president of the company, Charles E. Seiller, Jr., was able to identify an untapped audience for movies — working-class families which attended films only once or twice a year, although this market comprises more than 75% of the U.S. population. Under Seiller's system the audience practically designed every aspect of the movie itself. Each month researchers were sent around the country "to question potential moviegoers on unusual ideas, newspaper articles, current books, or anything that might get them out of the house and into the theater" (Morrisroe, 1980). Eventually, even these sophisticated techniques could not save Sunn Classic Pictures, as they fell victim to the problems of distribution caused by competition from the major studios, but their experiences taught the whole industry to be conscious of the potential of scientific audience research.

The title of a movie is important for obvious reasons; it forms the initial stimulus on the part of the audience to want to see a movie. Therefore, it is not surprising that movie companies are busy researching titles in order to assess not only their effectiveness, but also to understand what connotations they convey. Most of the major studios have hired advertising agencies to run the campaigns for movies, and this includes title testing. An agency advised Columbia Pictures that the enigmatic title *The China Syndrome,* although obscure, was also "more provocative" and "more memorable" than alternatives such as *Eyewitness* or *Power* (Honeycutt, 1979). The techniques used to test titles include lengthy in-home interviews. In questioning moviegoers, researchers try several approaches, ranging from sampling the "want-to-see factor" to a free-association test in which the person being interviewed is given a movie's title and stars and then asked to describe what he or she thinks the movie is about.

Austin (1989:Chapter 4) has identified a wide range of factors which constitute the "elements in the movie attendance process." These include factors surrounding the production (director, producer, studio), advertising and publicity, story type, and personal and impersonal influences. Studios now test market their advertising strategies before launching their campaigns, adjusting the "selling proposition" of the movie according to their research findings in an attempt to convince the potential audience that its needs and gratifications will be satisfied by viewing this particular film. Of course, even the use of such sophisticated techniques does not guarantee success, as audience preferences are notoriously difficult to predict with any certainty. (For a history of the problem of audience preference research see Jowett, 1985).

Several researchers have noted the particular significance of previews (known as "trailers" because in the early movie period they came at the end of the show, not at the beginning as they do today) in the successful marketing of movies. Faber and O'Guinn (1984:373) note that: "A preview can be considered a form of direct prior experience since it is an actual interaction with a small portion of a specific film and occurs in the normal movie going environment." Austin (1989:68) points out that: "Anecdotal reports indicating that many people do not perceive trailers as a form of advertising [which, of course, they are] but rather view them as an opportunity to learn about a film heighten the importance of trailers. They are free from the self-serving connotations of other forms of advertising." Faber and O'Guinn (1984) also found that previews were judged as the most useful source of information about the actual film, ranking above other sources such as interpersonal contact, critics' reviews and media advertising, In contrast to other forms of advertising, the preview is the one which is able to present information about a film in the most visual and entertaining manner.

Other than previews, studios have resorted to "fine-honing" their product before releasing it by previewing a completed version of the film to real audiences in selected test sites. Today it is a rare major motion picture that is not tested before general release. Currently (1988), an international firm called National Research Group handles the screen testings of two-thirds of all the movies released in the United States. NRG charges from $2,000 to $8,000 per test in rough form for specifically recruited audiences, or for a lesser fee will conduct preview testing of a more final form at designated theaters, with a normal cross-sectional audience. The results of these tests "are used primarily by the filmmaker to shape his picture; the later screenings are employed more for the benefit of the film company's marketing department" (Siskel, 1986). Using the results of audience testing can help a studio match the final film with the target audience, and determine the advertising strategy to be used; but even these techniques cannot always ensure that movies will attain their predicted box office potential when they are released. Given the wide range of factors which can influence an audience to attend a movie at a given point in time, it is impossible to predict its actual performance in the marketplace with consistent accuracy.

The problem with many of these techniques, their critics claim, is that one need know nothing about movies to utilize them, a fact which many Hollywood veterans deplore as it removes the mystique associated with being able to judge the audience's needs, upon which their reputations often depend. Nevertheless, as the cost of production continues to increase, more and more empirical research is being done by the movie studios as a means of recouping their investments. How far one can develop quasi-scientific theories about something as amorphous as "the movie business" remains to be seen. There is little doubting, however, that as the competition for the box office dollar continues we will see the development of still more sophisticated techniques in an attempt to understand the fickle audience.

ALTERNATIVE EXPLANATIONS

The manner in which a movie is viewed by the audience, essentially what the audience "takes away" from the movie, is a subject of much interest and conjecture, and several competing theories exist to explain it. As Monaco (1977:125) notes: "Film is not a language, but it is like a language, and since it is like a language, some of the methods that we use to study language might profitably be applied to a study of film." This basically linguistic approach to film has shown considerable growth in the last decade, especially the approach known as semiology, the study of the systems of signs. Seminal to this approach is the work of French researcher Christian Metz (1974), which has found favor with a wide variety of film scholars, especially those who write for the British magazine *Screen*. As Andrew (1976:217) explains:

It is the internal study of the mechanics of films themselves which Metz and his followers elect to investigate. Semiology in general is the science of meaning and film semiotics proposes to construct a comprehensive model capable of explaining how film embodies meaning or signifies it to an audience. It hopes to determine the laws which make the viewing of film possible and to uncover the particular patterns of signification which give individual films or genres their special character.

Thus, the semiologist is interested essentially only in the film itself, leaving aspects of audience interaction, location, and even psychological predispositions to others.

While it is impossible to do full justice to the semiological study of film in a text such as this, certain basic concepts essential to the semiologist can be clarified. First, semiologists work with "codes," by which they mean "the logical relationship which allows a message to be understood. . . . [T]hey are the rules which allow the messages of a film [to exist]" (Andrew, 1976:224). These codes, constructed by the semiologist, allow the movie to be broken down in such a way as to indicate the specificity of meaning, the generalizations which may be possible from such meanings, and the possible further reduction to subcodes. As Andrew (1976:225-226) notes: "One of the primary tasks of the film semiologist is the enumeration of the kinds of codes appearing in a film or in certain groups of films, and the determination of the various levels of specificity of these codes." The code can be specific to one movie, or it can be traced historically across a series of movies, but the encoding of the screen image is central to the work of the semiologist.

Another key element in the semiological study of movies is the concept of the film as a "text." In fact, the semiologist is not limited to a single movie as his text, but may take a unit as small as a single sequence or as large as an entire genre of movies. The codes in turn are examined within the text, as this is "capable of conferring a value on messages" (Andrew, 1976:227).

There are currently many other competing theories of explanation of "meaning" of movie content and its effect on the audience. Such explanations range over a continuum from largely empirical on one side, to the highly imaginative and speculative use of semiology and structuralist approaches on the other. As an example of the first is the more traditional form of content analysis, in which the frequency and direction of occurrence is used as basis for making connections between the manifest content of the films and the observable social and cultural tensions in the society that created them. (For an example see Linton and Jowett, 1977.) In the middle would be a form of content analysis (or more precisely, sampling), combined with introspective evaluations of the symbolic significance of what appeared on the screen as a means of determining the relationship between a society and its films. Such studies go beyond mere description of the manifest content, attempting to reveal hidden, or latent meanings. (Examples of these types of analytical/ descriptive techniques are Biskind, 1983; Polan, 1986; and Sayre, 1982). At the far end of the continuum is the growing number of studies using variations of semiology, structuralism or, increasingly, psychoanalytic theories to get at the real meaning of what appears on the screen and the audience's reception of this latent content. (Examples of such studies are found throughout various editions of the British Journal *Screen;* see also the variety of methods used in the essays in Nichols, 1985.)

Semiologist and others attempting to get beneath the surface meanings of movie content have been accused of being unnecessarily obscure, and this criticism may be justified. However, in their defense it should be pointed out that they are trying to go beyond the surface meanings of movie messages, and this often involves the use of a language specifically created for this purpose. This "metalanguage" and the difficulty in articulating the concepts involved to the uninitiated has tended to separate the semiological approach from the historically accepted mainstream of film analysis. Perhaps in the near future a greater degree of accessibility will encourage more social scientists to be receptive to the semiological approach, for it obviously has much to offer as we struggle to understand how movies influence their audiences.

The whole question of the relationship between the growth of interest in film theory and an interest in what role the movies play as a recognized institution within the general social structure is best summarized by Monaco (1977):

> People who think about film are no longer content simply to describe an ideal system of esthetics or political and social values, nor do they see their main aim finding a language to describe the phenomenon of film. The job of film theory now is profoundly dialectical: cinema is an enormous and far-reaching set of interrelating oppositions: between filmmaker and subject, film and observer, establishment and avant garde . . . culture and society . . . a never ending set of codes and subcodes that raises fundamental questions about the relationship of life and art, reality and language.

PSYCHOANALYSIS AND MOVIE ANALYSIS

The movies, as indicated earlier, have often been seen as analogous to dreams, and it was for this reason that the famed social worker Jane Addams called the movie theater the "Dream Palace" in recognition of the role of the earlier movies for the urban working class. The movies operate as "dreams" in several different ways: First, through fantasy they can fulfill the dreams of the audience. They can also act in a deeper psychological sense to symbolize our hidden fears and desires, and thus act as a form of "conscious dreaming." Finally, movies can act as a source for our real dreams, especially where there might be strong identification with a movie star or a specific incident. (An example of this can be found in the enormous influence of *The Exorcist* on many of the people who saw it. There were many reports that individuals were emotionally disturbed for substantial periods after viewing the movie.)

In one of the more important works which utilizes theories of psychoanalysis to examine movies, Wolfenstein and Leites (1950:11) noted that "Day-dreams contain clues to deeper-lying, less articulate aspirations, fears and wishes . . . [and] . . . day-dreams provide the starting point for literary and dramatic productions." The importance of this concept for movies is that movies can become the "shared day-dream" for millions of people, for "where a group of people share a common culture, they are likely to have certain day-dreams in common" (Wolfenstein and Leites, 1950:13). Thus, movies can serve as a kind of collective unconsciousness, inspiring, creating tensions, and almost causing a "standardization" of fantasy. Movies can create ideals of the perfect male or female, or perhaps provide an agenda for the ideal lifestyle, all of which is unwittingly ingested by the viewer.

In recent years psychoanalytic theories of film have been widely used in the emerging field of feminist film criticism, which attempts to examine how women have been portrayed in the movies. The theories of Freud and their elaborate recastings by French psychoanalyst Jacques Lacan have been used to identify and explain the essential "maleness" perspective of most movies. In her important examination of this topic, Laura Mulvey (Nichols, 1985:305) pointedly noted: "Psychoanalytic theory is thus appropriated here as a political weapon, demonstrating the way the unconscious of patriarchal society has structured film form." Dudley Andrew (1984:157-158) has pointed out that psychoanalysts differ profoundly in their conception of the relationship between symbols or "signs" in films and their meanings for audiences. Nevertheless, there is continued interest in using psychoanalytic theories as part of the ongoing process to get at these real (or latent) meanings.

Parker Tyler, one of the pioneers in the use of what he called the "psychoanalytic-mythological" method of movie analysis, noted that

Hollywood is the mass unconscious — scooped up as crudely as a steam shovel scoops up the depths of a hill, and served on a helplessly empty screen. A thousand small wishes are symbolically satisfied by the humblest and the worst Hollywood movie, and the excellence or triteness of a movie has little to do with satisfying the average customer [Tyler, 1944].

THE ROLE OF THE MOVIES

Exactly what is the function of the movies in modern society? Why do people continue to attend what should be by now an almost technologically redundant medium in a world where audiovisual images can be much more easily and cheaply obtained? Several theories have been advanced: Some have seen the movies primarily as "entertainment" (Quigley, 1947), while others have been more concerned with their latent effects as a reflector of the stress patterns and the commensurate needs of their audience (Houseman, 1947).

Haley (1952) examined the theory that people went to movies primarily to "get away from their problems," and he suggested that "people attend movies more often, and in larger numbers, during economic crises and wars. . . . This anxiety must be relieved by some interpretation or form of reassurance." He pointed out that movie attendance had increased following the stock-market collapse in 1929 and again during World War II, and that the unexpected increase in 1951 could have been due to the outbreak of hostilities in Korea. Thus, movie attendance could act as an indicator of tensions in society. Haley further suggested that as the traditional family structure disintegrated, there would be a greater reliance by young people on all the mass media to "provide an interpretation [of life] which was once the province of family and cultural traditions" (Haley, 1952:374).

Clearly movies continue to play an important role in the leisure pattern of our society. Recent theories about moviegoing, although developed from a wide range of methodological and philosophical perspectives, do not really offer a definitive explanation for the continued interest in and attendance at movies. Bruce Austin, in his detailed examination of the literature on movie audience (Austin 1989), makes a strong case for understanding moviegoing as a model based on the interaction between audience expectancies and the fulfillment of gratifications. In simple terms, the audience believes that by going to a particular movie, it will receive some sort of satisfaction of its need to be entertained. (It should be emphasized that not everyone finds gratification from going to the movies, and attendance falls off dramatically with age and education.) The quest for closer identification with a star or story, the desire for social contact, the need for diversion, or even the sheer wish to get in out of the cold or heat are all valid reasons for going to the movies. But surely it is also more than that, for movies strike a deeper note in our psyches. They continue to provide vivid images and to fuel our dreams. The movie is an enigmatic social and cultural entity, an entertainment form which survives ephemera, a diversion which often transcends time, and a social force often ignored by those concerned with social change. The movies are much more than they seem.

5

THE HOLLYWOOD VERSION
The Socio-Cultural and Political Effects of the Movies

The movies are a worldwide cultural influence. When a new form of communication is introduced into a society, it causes major shifts in the way that society perceives itself. The interrelationship between a society and its movies is complex, but careful analysis can reveal a great deal about social and cultural tensions. The movies, as witnessed by an examination of the Depression era, go beyond being only entertainment, but fill other needs in the society. Movies also have been used for both blatant and subtle attempts to propagandize. Culturally, the movies have been very important in shaping our "visual" perspective.

In 1921 English writer Arthur Weigall (1921:668) noted:

> To the remotest towns of England, as to those of America and other countries, these films penetrate, carrying with them this mild but ultimately dangerous poison; and gradually the world, from end to end, is being trained to see life as it is seen by a certain group of kinema [movie] producers and writers congregated in a corner of the United States. The world is being Americanised by the photoplay; but the trouble is that this Americanisation does not represent the best element of that nation, or even the most popular.

Once the movies became a popular worldwide phenomenon, such sentiments were often voiced by those concerned with the supposed influence of this new entertainment medium. (For a detailed treatment of the emergence of the movies as an "unexpected" social and cultural force in the interwar period, see Jowett, 1986.) Much of their fear had to do with the fact that after the devastation wrought by World War I, the American movie industry quickly moved to fill the gap, and the Hollywood industry dominated European and worldwide movie screen time (Guback, 1969; Street, 1985; Swann, 1987). This movie hegemony was so serious that many countries attempted at various times to impose quotas on American movies, or to force an agreed-upon rate of movie exchanges. The former proved difficult to enforce and did not solve the outward flow of currency, while any attempt to arrange an exchange of "foreign" movies was doomed because American audiences simply disliked non-American movies. (This was in the silent era, when the problem of language had not yet emerged!) The problem was a very real one, for in 1926 the Hollywood industry claimed that "an average of about seventy-five percent of the motion pictures shown day in and day out the world over are of American origin" (North, 1926:100).

What was the effect of the advent of the movies as a major entertainment, social, and cultural force? This question can also be asked of the other forms of mass communication. It is a sad academic fact that despite all the volumes of research on the question of mass media "effects" we are still a long way from dealing with one important historical mystery. How have the various forms of mass communication altered the way we both communicate and perceive the world around us? While he is no longer as intellectually fashionable as he once was, media philosopher Marshall McLuhan (1966) addressed this question when he suggested that alterations in the communications framework would also alter the "sense ratio" of a society, by which he meant the tools used by the society to examine and understand itself. This, unlike many other McLuhanesque "probes," is a highly significant and fundamental question; and yet it is one which has not captured the attention of scholars in a way which has led to any real breakthroughs in our understanding of how changes in the communications infrastructure (we could also call this "the flow of information") actually cause changes in the society and its culture.

The role of the dominant channels of information in shaping the way each society perceives itself is of fundamental importance in understanding which perceptions leave the greatest imprint on a culture. Thus, the moves from oral to script, from script to print, and finally from print to various forms of audiovisual modes of communication have each caused an observable shift in the manner in which information (and therefore ideas) moves in a society (Jowett, 1975). Perhaps of greater significance, the advent of a new mode of communication, such as the movies, also alters the basic way the society perceives itself. In altering the balance between the various forms of communication, the introduction of a new channel of information also restructures the agenda of those things which we deem to be important.

An obvious example of this type of cultural restructuring would be in a society where the visual media (movies and especially television) have become the dominant forms of communication. In this case the authentic, public "visual experience" becomes more important than the more personal, internal "mind images" created by written material. While such shifts are obvious, few historians or sociologists of literature or the mass media have bothered to examine what this type of fundamental shift means to a society. (For more information on this topic see Eisenstein, 1979; and Havelock, 1963).

For a student of the movies the shift in the dominant paradigm from print to visual stimuli is of great importance. Putting it at its simplest, if the major form of public entertainment shifts away from relying on personalized mental images (reading or listening) to relying on graphic and vivid images created and standardized by outside agencies, how does this affect the whole nature of the cultural experience in that society? If the entire population is subjected to these same standardized images, what effect does this ultimately have on the culture? These basic but neglected questions deserve more intellectual respect and inquiry. While the answers may not be easy to obtain, at the very least, this problem and all that it suggests about the role of the mass media in our lives should be firmly lodged in our minds.

MOVIES AND SOCIETY: SOME CONCEPTUAL AND METHODOLOGICAL PROBLEMS

The question of the effect the introduction of the movies as a new form of information (as well as being an entertainment) has on our society needs much further investigation (see Chapter 3). More specifically, those who study movies in the sociocultural context need to absorb much of the empirical findings which have come out of the field of communication studies and apply it to the question of "movie influence." Such systematic analysis would also diminish the unfortunate tendency among movie historians to repeat constantly the anecdotes about isolated incidents of movie influence, such as the famous story of Clark Gable's bare chest in the movie *It Happened One Night* (1934) causing the sales of men's undershirts to decline drastically. Of much greater importance is the long-term but constant exposure of the audience to certain kinds of "messages," whether they be as subtle as Hollywood's vision of domestic furniture designs (any Fred Astaire-Ginger Rogers movie) or as blatant as one of the anti-communist movies of the 1950s (*My Son John* is a good example of this genre).

This is where the question of the interrelationship between a society and its movies really lies. We should be under no illusions that such research is easy, or that results can be readily obtained. What is clearly needed is a better research method aimed at examining the nature of the "message" delivered in movies. This leads to a whole series of equally important secondary questions. What are the roles and functions of those who create the movie? Who is responsible for conception of the original idea, and what metamorphosis does the entire concept undergo from start to finish? Essentially, we need to know why *this* project was selected from all the myriad available projects and what public nerve it was supposed to touch. This will allow us to contrast the creator's perceptions of what the public wants (needs?) with demonstrable public attitudes. In recent years, there has been increased interest in examining "the production of culture" as an aspect of popular culture studies. This body of work sees "cultural products and practices in terms of the relations between their material conditions of existence and their work as representations which produce meanings" (Barrett et al., 1979). Thus the ideological position of the creator of the movie, the particular structure of the entire motion picture industry, and even the audience's predispositions all contribute to the "meaning" of the film on the screen.

If such examinations are undertaken within the framework of the prevailing historical-cultural context, the results should be a rich field for film scholars and others interested in the role and function of the mass media. It will open the doors for assessing the way various aspects of the popular culture (not just the movies) contribute to the formation of public attitudes, and it will do much toward giving the entire field of popular culture studies renewed vigor. In particular, the role of the mass media in the creation of "ideology" has been given new credibility and prominence in recent years. As Stuart Hall (1982) has pointed out, there is now a renewed understanding of the mass media which has "raised them to a central, relatively independent, position" in any analysis of the formation of ideology in societies.

This question takes on even greater significance when we attempt to deal with a specific problem such as the assessment of the historical contribution of the movies to America (and worldwide) society in the twentieth century. Here we have some advantage in at least having some fairly objective historical trends available as a backdrop to the changing content of the movies. This, unfortunately, must be balanced against the lack of information available from the creators of the movies, although there exists within the untapped files of the studios an immense wealth of useful information. It has only been in the last decade that scholars have been able to gain access to the actual files of the motion picture studios and the various agencies of the MPAA, particularly the Production Code Administration, which acted as the moral "watchdog" for the industry. This has resulted in some significant new interpretations about the way in which the Hollywood industry worked, and how these practices shaped the product seen on the screen. (An excellent example of this "revisionist" work is Gomery, 1986 which reconceptualizes many of our notions about the Hollywood studio system.)

Historical trends in content contrasted with shifts in public tastes and values are only now being studied once again, after a hiatus of nearly three decades while television occupied center stage for communications researchers. We may be closer to achieving some real understanding of the way in which movies and society interact.

MOVIES AND SOCIETY: THE MOVIE-MADE CULTURE

There are many possible influences which can shape the culture or the way of life of a society. We have already established that the movies have been one of the factors to be taken into account when we try to list such influences. It was perhaps in the period 1929-1947 that the movies as a way of life in

Table 5.1 U.S. Motion Picture Box Office Receipts in Relation to Personal
Consumption Expenditures

Date	Admissions ($Millions)	Percentage Total Recreational Expenditures	Percentage Total Spectator Amusement Expenditures
1929	720	16.62	78.86
1933	482	21.89	84.12
1937	672	19.99	82.64
1941	809	19.08	81.31
1944	1,341	24.73	85.80
1946	1,692	19.81	81.90
1970	1,629	3.84	49.42
1975	2,197	3.13	50.89
1980	2,671	2.32	41.16
1982	3,326	2.40	42.65
1985	3,676	2.22	38.04

SOURCES: U.S. Department of Commerce, *Statistical Abstract of the United States, 1987,* Table #365; and Jowett (1976), Appendices.

America reached its peak; and examination of the movies in Depression America affords us an opportunity to understand something about the way the medium had become an integral part of social and cultural life.

The fact that sound movies were introduced at the precise time that an economic depression was taking hold proved to be a short-lived happy coincidence for the movie industry. The novelty of sound kept audience numbers artificially inflated between 1929 and 1931, when attendance suddenly declined from the 1930 high of 90 million attendances per week. As can be seen from Table 5.1, the box office dollar showed very definite declines in 1931 and only recovered after 1940, when wartime conditions increased movie attendance. Of much greater significance, however, is the movies' percentage of the "Total Personal Consumption Expenditures" and "Total Recreational Expenditures," which indicates that movies played an increasingly important role in recreational pursuits during the period until 1947.

The fact that movies continued to survive (and quite well compared with other industries) was not lost upon social critics. James Rorty (1935:162) noted:

> The [movie] industry is more necessary, hence more stable, than steel or housing or power. . . . Indeed, the suffering and bewilderment of the depression augmented the demand for dreams, in so far as it became less and less possible for the average person to master or adjust to the intolerable realities of disemployment and destitution.

This was also true of the other major mass medium of the 1930s— radio. Erik Barnouw (1968:6) pointed out that "according to social workers, destitute families that had to give up an icebox or furniture or bedding still clung to the radio as to a last link with humanity." Clearly, the nation was turning to the mass media not only for news and information, but also for entertaining relief from an oppressive economic situation.

What were average Americans learning from the movies they saw during this period? While it is difficult to make sweeping generalizations because movie content was so diverse, nevertheless some overall attitudes and values were communicated. After his extensive analysis of Depression-era movies, Andrew Bergman (1971:167-168) noted:

> The movies made a central contribution toward educating Americans in the fact that wrongs could be set right within their existing institutions. They did so not by haunting the screen with bogeyman Reds but . . . by reflecting aspiration and achievement. They showed that individual initiative still bred success, that the federal government was a benevolent watchman, that we were a classless, melting pot nation.

Thus, gangster films, musicals, "screwball comedies," melodramas, westerns, and adventure films all contributed in varying degrees to the overall ethos of the period. Some critics read more into these movies than others, but those who were there remember the movies as important social experiences. Writing in the 1960s, John Clellon Holmes (1965:51) suggested that it was not so much World War II that was the major socializing influence on his generation. Instead,

> everyone who is now between the ages of thirty-odd and forty-odd had already shared a common experience by the time they entered the armed services. It was the experience of moviegoing in the 1930s and early 1940s, and it gave us all a fantasy life in common, from which we are still dragging up the images that obsess us . . . for the movies of the 1930s constitute, for my generation, nothing less than a kind of Jungian collective consciousness, a decade of coming attractions out of which some of the truths of our maturity have been formed.

We can read similar comments from other writers who were able to articulate their reactions to movies, but what about the millions of moviegoers who were influenced by what they saw, who internalized the messages but never really understood or cared where the sources for their ideas came from? Movies, like all the mass media, serve as a potent source of informal education, and thus their content, no matter how innocuous it may appear, is never entirely free of value judgments or even of ideological or political biases. The commercial movie industry has historically gone out of its way to claim that it has no political or ideological axes to grind, but as Linton (1978) has suggested,

> popular U.S. films operate as dramas of reassurance. The beliefs, attitudes and values presented in Hollywood films tend to resonate with the dominant beliefs, attitudes and values of American society. In other words, the domi-

nant ideology of a society tends to be reinforced by the ideology presented in its films.

This ideological bias of movie content is more obvious when movies are exported to countries with a differing viewpoint, and it is likely to cause friction if the differences are too severe. Even a country as similar in value structure to the United States as Canada has had strong reactions to certain American movies in the past (Berton, 1975; Jowett, 1977). The export of a cultural (ideological) perspective is particularly exacerbated when it is accompanied by an equally pervasive form of economic domination. The sheer size and enormous popularity of the American movie industry gives it a decided advantage when it competes in the world market, but, as was previously noted, the "point of view" of American films is not always welcomed (Schiller, 1969, 1973, 1976; Tunstall, 1977). (The issue of "cultural imperialism" and American mass communication, especially film, is discussed extensively in Jowett, 1986; Schiller, 1969, 1973, 1976; Street, 1985; Swann, 1987; Tunstall, 1977.)

While we have been discussing the persuasive content of what are on the surface essentially entertainment movies, there have been many attempts to use movies as both subtle and blatant propaganda. In general, blatant attempts to propagandize through the medium of the entertainment movie have not been successful; the communication of ideas, attitudes, and values is much more likely if the intent of the moviemaker is not clear. Thus, early during World War II, when Hollywood was criticized for not making films with a strong propagandistic flavor, producer Walter Wanger (1939) noted that 120,000 prints of American movies were circulating in overseas markets and that these were the most direct American "ambassadors" to the rest of the world. The typical Hollywood movie was an important channel for informing the rest of the world about the American "way of life" with the stress on entertainment rather than overt proselytizing.

It appears as if movie audiences are too conditioned to the structure of the typical Hollywood narrative film to accept obvious propagandistic content. (Of course, the level of susceptibility to propaganda can vary from culture to culture according to the type of political system.) Also the structure of the film production and distribution industries make it extremely difficult for those outside of the mainstream to use the system for propaganda purposes. As a recent book on propaganda (Jowett and O'Donnell, 1986:81-82) pointed out:

The motion picture's effectiveness as a propaganda medium is now totally limited to the values and ideologies that are an integral part of the plot structure. Such content, although subtle, is in its own right an extremely potent source of modern propaganda, and is certainly more powerful in the long run than the deliberate and often clumsy attempts in the past.

The more blatant attempts to use movies for deliberate attempts to persuade have met with varying results. The empirical research on the subject indicates that movies rarely cause any strong changes in attitude (Furhammer and Isaksson, 1971). However, it should be kept in mind that the instruments of measurement in these cases are often unable to detect the subtlety of alteration which may take place when audiences are exposed to messages of a uniform nature with a constantly repeated value structure. Thus, most of the research on movie influence (see Austin, 1987; Jowett, 1976:369-373) deals with individual movies, but it is the cumulative effect of years of viewing movies which so far defies adequate measurement and which is of real interest in any assessment of the movies' impact on society and culture.

THE MOVIES AND MATERIAL CULTURE

Movies have made a considerable contribution to those artifacts in society which we can call "the material culture." Because of their strong (although persuasively subtle) visual influence, it is only natural to expect the movies to have contributed to the visual aspects of modern culture. In this manner movies have served as an initiator of certain styles of cultural expression such as clothes, hair fashions, and even manners of speech; but they have also served as a conduit for the spreading of less well-known ideas of forms of expression. This latter point is amply demonstrated by the less-than-subtle use of modernist painting influences in German films such as *The Cabinet of Dr. Caligari* or the pervasive use of "Art Moderne" styles in the RKO films of Fred Astaire and Ginger Rogers.

There are more obvious and ubiquitous examples of this type of movie influence. Who would have thought that Marlon Brando's characterization in *The Wild One* would influence succeeding generations of motorcycle gangs as it has? This characterization was based upon Brando's own careful observations, but his screen persona was so powerful and attractive that his depiction has become a persistent role model for those who participate in this form of subculture. Few screen images have had such a degree of longevity as these influences.

In a less obvious sense the movies color our perception of our own history (Jowett, 1970). Thus, certain periods of American history are emphasized in the popular culture to an extreme, such as the short period of western expansion between 1865-1880, while other equally significant periods (of perhaps greater historical importance, in fact) are ignored; the period of the American Revolution is an obvious example. The reason for such skewing is that Hollywood simply found a greater opportunity for the creation of a dramatic, conventional narrative, and at a lower cost, in the formulaic western than in the more or less authentic recreation of the Revolutionary period. Also, the opportunity for dramatic license is much less in the well-established facts surrounding the Revolution. (As a clear demonstration of this, the movie *Revolution* (1986), despite having a very popular star in Al Pacino, and a lavish production from a studio which had recently won an academy award for *Chariots of Fire,* failed both artistically and at the box office. Much of the criticism of the movie centered around the lack of "drama" in the film!)

What would be more authentic than the actual historical facts are the visual aspects of the narrative, the costumes, hairstyles, and other props; although here, too, stylistic license is often taken. (The height of cowboy hats in modern westerns has been reduced considerably for aesthetic reasons from the actual height used in the late nineteenth century.) The movie thus becomes a quasi-encyclopedia in which one finds the visual repository of much of our culture. This can easily be demonstrated if one closes one's eyes and tries to visualize in as much detail as possible a historical figure such as the Roman Centurion. Think. Where did this image originate? In most cases it would be either the movies or television. In our society very few individuals would cite a book as the source.

The fact that movies directly influence our visual repository has not been sufficiently considered when the issue of "influence" is discussed. Earlier, the question of the standardization of these images was raised, and here too we need to consider the combination of visual power and repetition. As an example, how do the movies depict women? Is the image of women in the 1980s movie different from that found in the 1930s? Which is more pervasive? One could make a strong case that the longevity of many "classic" films of the 1930s allows and even encourages the persistence of these older images. If these are repeated and standardized, they easily become stereotypes; this is how many of our stereotypes of women (or men) are created and constantly reinforced (Haskell, 1973; Mellen, 1978). Feminist film criticism has become a recognized approach to the study of film in the last decade, and this has provided extensive documentation about the essential "maleness" of most movie production. However, given the historical structure of the movie industry, it is unlikely that there will be a dramatic shift toward a more feminist perspective in commercial films in the near future. Nevertheless, feminist film criticism has sensitized male filmmakers, and as more women become filmmakers themselves, there is bound to be a move toward a middle position. (The issues which incorporate the feminist perspective on film are discussed in Doanne et al., 1984; Kaplan, 1983.)

The material culture is directly affected by the images created and fostered by the movies, for they provide a type of visual shorthand with which we are easily able to identify individuals or groups. Thus, gangsters are Italian; all Frenchmen (or Frenchwomen) are amorous by nature; all Germans are robust, blond, and stern; and all Englishmen are befuddled and well-bred. These images are commonplace in the popular culture as a whole, but they take on added significance in the movies because of their strong visual reinforcement. Thus, when we read about similar stereotypical characters, or listen to the rare radio drama, we visualize them in cinematic terms. Even if we are not frequent moviegoers, the movie-made images are so powerful that they form a corner-stone in the mind. The movies are always with us.

6

"YOU AIN'T HEARD [AND SEEN] NOTHIN' YET"

The Future of Theatrical Movies

While the death of Hollywood has been announced a number of times, the movies have demonstrated an unwillingness to disappear. Other than the doomsayers, however, very few people have attempted to speculate on what the future holds for theatrical movies. Moreover, those who speculate have often done so "off the top of their heads" without considering technological, demographic, and economic projections. When technological developments in the movies and competitive media are considered, along with the age and education distributions of future populations, and when the possibilities with regard to economic arrangements are added in, the future of theatrical movies remains basically uncertain. Nevertheless, it has been noted that audience losses to the new technologies seem to have been offset by increased moviegoing by older, better educated and more affluent patrons, and many analysts feel there is a "core" audience which will always make theatrical movies a viable first "window" of exhibition.

"PREDICTING" THE FUTURE

In discussing a survey among American movie critics published in *Film 67/68,* Jerzy Toeplitz (1974:243) noted "a remarkable reluctance to speculate about the future" of the movies. He explained this reluctance as a consequence of these writers' roles within the daily and weekly presses which forced them to focus on "immediate rather than general issues." Basically, Toeplitz understood this hesitation since such conjecture required an overview of the entire culture and the role that the movies occupy within it (and might occupy as the culture responds to change).

The history of the movies might also discourage speculation about their future. First of all, movies have always demonstrated a lack of concern (or very little concern) for anything except the present. As Axel Madsen (1975:163) observes: "The movies have always lived as if there were no tomorrow, and no yesterday." Second, movies have managed to disprove predictions of the industry's demise in the past, as a result of what appears to be a series of "regular miracles" brought about by technological innovations (Fadiman, 1973). Sound, color and the wide screen helped at one point when movies were struggling, but the aid which each brought was ultimately short-lived, suggesting "that Hollywood is in constant need of assistance from some outside source" (Fadiman, 1973:146). A third factor deterring specula-tion about the future of movies is related to this dependence on technological innovation.

The most recent developments that have had a tremendous impact on movies are ones related to video technology, particularly those involving viewer-controlled, video record-and-playback equipment (i.e., VCRs, video-discs, etc.). The pace of innovation and the struggle for market control among companies producing basically incompatible devices initially infused the whole area with considerable volatility and uncertainty, although subsequent events introduced a modicum of stability after an initial "shakeout" of weaker competitors — a pattern often repeated during the introduction of technologi-cal innovations.

As Edmunds and Strick (1977:159) have pointed out, for example, in the early phase of this competition among video media, "There are or have been at least 25 video-disc systems, all but one of which was developed since 1970." Moreover, the two video systems which Peter Guber (1972) was touting at the beginning of the 1970s as the leading contenders for market dominance (CBC's EVR and Avco's Cartravision) were dropped in 1973 at a cost of $50 million to each developer (Edmunds and Strick, 1977). Subsequent developments were to sound a virtual death knell for the videodisc as a commercially competitive, entertainment-delivery technology although in the late 1980s there appears to be renewed interest as a result of the growth of audio compact discs, and a significant improvement in the basic technology.

A perhaps more fundamental difficulty has been an attitude in general human affairs that is analogous to the one exhibited in the movie industry. "It is hard to think seriously about the future because we take the present so much for granted," writes Leo Bogart (1968:409). While this observation may have a great deal of validity, a growing segment of society has become concerned about the nature of the future in which we and our descendants will live. Perhaps spurred by the developments in space exploration, demographic projections of overpopulation, the depletion of natural resources, the dangers of pollution, and the threat of nuclear annihilation, concerned individuals around the world began to make concerted efforts in the 1960s to develop techniques to explore the future — and perhaps develop methods to influence its course. American futurology (or "futurism" or "futuristics") had its origins in basically two developments: the setting up of the Commission on the Year

2000 by the American Academy of Arts and Sciences in 1965 and the establishment of the World Future Society at about the same time (Ferkiss, 1977). This "modern futurology combines the knowledge of the scientist, the will of the utopian, and the imagination of the writer of science fiction" (Ferkiss, 1977:6).

While some such thinkers have turned their attention to communications in general (and telecommunications particularly), none of them seems to have explored the future of the theatrical movie in any great detail. Martin (1977), in "A Future Scenario," for example, concentrates on the electronic media and only briefly observes that by the 1990s public movie theaters will have declined as a result of competition from home entertainment and will exhibit basically two kinds of movies: sex-related movies too explicit for the home market and those which utilize technological capabilities (180° or 360° screens) unavailable with the home technology. A more detailed examination of the movies' future was undertaken by Spraos (1962). However, his study of the British theatrical situation differed greatly from general futurist studies. First, his time frame was considerably shorter than futurists tend to employ: From the perspective of the early 1960s, he was projecting the state of moviegoing in Britain in 1970. Second, his approach explicitly ruled out consideration of possibly relevant, new technologies—an element which futurists see as central in social causation (Ferkiss, 1977).

Spraos' neglect of possible new technologies resulted from his contracted time frame rather than a devaluation of the potential role of technology. In the analysis that he developed, however, Spraos would seem to have followed Bogart's (1968) suggestion that economic, cultural, and political factors must be considered in addition to the strictly technological when contemplating future developments in the realm of media. In the speculations that follow concerning the future of theatrical movies, then, a number of factors have been considered: possible technological developments in movies (especially innovations in theatrical display), as well as in other related media; changes in the size and demographics of the population at large, and of the movie audience in particular; and economic trends which could be expected to have some impact on movies and their place in the social order. It should be borne in mind, however, that what is presented below are not predictions, but rather *suggestions* as to what could happen in the future given the perspective of the present situation.

THE MOVIES' RELATIONSHIP TO TELEVISION

The introduction of television is generally regarded as the primary reason for the decline in movie attendance following the record years of the 1940s. It took the movie industry years to recover from this decline and to readjust to the fact that movies were no longer the main entertainment medium in North America. Once this new equilibrium had been established, however, the majors were able to exploit the opportunities provided by this new competitive medium, both producing series and programs designed primarily for television exhibition and by selling the networks the television rights to their theatrical motion pictures. As continuing practices, the former strategy provides revenue and employment and injects a degree of continuity into overall production activities since the television and movie "seasons" tend to alternate rather than overlap.

The sale of movie rights to TV was also a lucrative source of revenue for many years. In the early 1970s, the networks were consuming about 400 movies a year including reruns, virtually stripping the vaults of the major studios (Fadiman, 1973). By the end of that decade, broadcasters were paying very high prices for the rights to show recently produced movies *relatively* shortly after their theatrical release. ABC seemed to be the biggest spender in this regard, paying $16.5 million for *The Sting,* $18.5 million for *Close Encounters of the Third Kind,* and $25 million for *Jaws* and *Jaws II* — in all cases for multiple (usually three) showings (Pringle, 1979).

Not everyone saw this development as fundamentally beneficial for the movie industry, however. To Fadiman (1973) it constituted the depletion of an almost nonrenewable resource, given the reduction in production at that particular time period. In addition, he felt that such a practice placed too much emphasis on revenue from an industry by-product rather than primary product (theatrical movies), thereby violating "an elementary business principle." (Dramatic shifts of industry revenues in the 1980s from theatrical to nontheatrical sources — mainly videocassettes — basically invalidated this concern.) Furthermore, the network practice in the late 1970s of bidding for movies before their theatrical release was also seen as a mechanism that would shift bargaining power to (and therefore lower revenues from) the networks (Litman, 1979). At that point, then, these factors, combined with the possibility of production competition from the networks themselves, established TV as more of a competitor than it would have appeared to have been at first glance — having the potential to undercut the movie industry's recently established equilibrium.

A problem did arise in the 1980s, but not in the terms the developments of the 1970s would have suggested. The networks' attempts at theatrical productions were relatively unsuccessful and were cutback or discontinued altogether. The escalation of payments for movie TV rights was stopped as well. Given their increased pre-broadcast exposure via home video and cable TV, movies were less of an attraction for TV audiences, and their ratings fell. Networks also found made-for-TV movies a more economical expenditure than payment for rights to theatrical ones. Consequently the number of newer movies shown during prime time on network TV dropped significantly.

Employing their adaptability to changes in the environment that has led Harmetz (1988b) to characterize them as chameleon-like, the movie producer-distributors countered with what amounted to an "end run." The syndication

TV market had normally followed the network market in terms of the staging or playoff pattern of movie releases. Given the decline in interest on the part of networks, however, Hollywood moved to offer a series of first-run movie packages directly to independent TV stations (Rosenthal, 1987; *Television/ Radio Age*, 1986). The terms involved a myriad of arrangements related to level and form of remuneration and timing of broadcast, and by the late 1980s the degree of success of the approach was still uncertain. What was clear, however, was that the contribution of combined network and syndicated TV sales to total movie revenues had fallen to 7% from 14% at the beginning of the decade (Simon, 1987, 1988; Zacks, 1986).

DEVELOPMENTS IN VIDEO COMMUNICATION

Even more threatening to this industry equilibrium were certain technological developments in the electronics and telecommunications industries which began to make themselves felt in the 1970s. One thrust in this direction has been provided by the introduction of videocassettes and videodiscs, which gave the consumer greater control over the selection and utilization of program content. Described as "in-home delivery" systems, these two media eliminated the necessity of leaving the home for entertainment purposes just as television did; moreover, it liberated the viewer from the "tyranny" of broadcast television time schedules.

Videocassettes (the audiovisual equivalents of magnetic audio cassette recorders) have the capability to both record and play back. The recording, feature was especially troublesome to the movie industry since it was feared that this facility would increase the incidence of movie "piracy" greatly. In the late 1970s, the revenue losses in this area were estimated at being anywhere from $20 million to $100 million annually (Goffa, 1977). These fears seem to have been realized to a great extent, since estimates of such losses in the late 1980s escalated to the $700-800 million range — with some as high as $1 billion (Brennan, 1988; Thomas, 1987). In fact, the Betamax-Disney/MCA decision legitimized the practice of recording movies off-air for personal use and was one factor that helped divert potential revenue from the movie industry.

On the other hand, videodiscs (a type of audiovisual record album) are capable only of playback. One system, LVR (longitudinal video recorder), was somewhat analogous to eight-track audiocassettes and had both playback and record capabilities. This technology was unsuccessful in establishing itself, however, and videodiscs were left as a playback-only medium.

In the battle between these two video media, videocassettes had the benefit of longer running times, "browsing" features, and the basic appeal of record capability, but videodiscs produced a better-quality picture and were lower priced than videocassettes containing pre-recorded material. A U.S. Navy study in the 1970s had attempted to assess relative prospects for their success and concluded that

> if the cassette machine costs more than twice [the]videodisc, the disc would win out; if the disc cost more than two-thirds of the cassette, the record advantage would succeed. It appears that the disc will stabilize at about half the cost of the cassette machine and the EIAJ [Electronics Industries Association of Japan] predicts a market for both [Edmunds, 1979:113].

The accuracy of the Navy study's predictions was uneven: the disc machine did *not* stabilize at about half the cost of the cassette, but with the disc's cost above two-thirds that of the cassette, the record feature of the latter won the day. Although the videodisc medium did not disappear altogether, and in fact enjoyed somewhat of a renaissance in the late 1980s, its strengths seemed to be in the educational and industrial markets and not in the mass entertainment market — where videocassettes held sway and videodiscs were able only to maintain a "presence."

By the mid-1980s, the competition between the VHS and Beta videocassette formats had been decided in favor of the former. In 1986, Beta's share of the market had slipped to 2 or 3% while VHS captured 95% — the remainder going to the new 8mm format (Lachenbruch, 1986). A year later, Beta's share of the U.S. market had slipped to 1% (Lachenbruch, 1987), and Sony, by then the sole manufacturer of the format, virtually conceded defeat in early 1988 when it began selling VHS machines in Europe, although it continued to sell the Beta system in North America. Competition for dominance, however, merely shifted ground as manufacturers attempted to capture segments of the more-difficult-to-sell-to market by lowering prices and increasing quality and/or compactness and portability (especially in the burgeoning camcorder segment of the industry). VHS enhanced picture sharpness and detail with super-VHS (SVHS); Beta responded with ED (extended definition) Beta. On the smaller format front, Beta's proponents introduced 8mm equipment while the Japan Victor Corp. (JVC) countered with VHS-C ("compact"). All told, industry competition in the U.S. in 1985 saw 86 brands vying for sales, with the top 33 capturing 96.4% and the other 53 dividing the remainder. General Electric with its own and RCA brands led with almost 19%, followed by Matsushita's Panasonic and Quasar accounting for 16% (*Television Digest* survey cited in Lachenbruch, 1987).

While the outcome of these intraindustry competitions may not be of fundamental concern to theatrical motion pictures, the very existence of these new technologies *is:* Videocassettes (and to a limited extent, videodiscs) have fragmented and siphoned off the potential movie audience and threaten to increase their impact. Nielsen Media Research gauged VCR penetration at more then 50% in mid-1987, with levels above or near 60% for major urban markets such as Los Angeles, New York, and Chicago (Lachenbruch, 1987).

Estimates by the Electronics Industry Association (EIA) put the national rate at 52% in early 1988 (*Variety,* 1988), while the 1987 figure for Canada was 51% (Bureau of Broadcast Measurement data cited in (*Variety,* 1988b). EIA projected 1987 VCR sales of almost 13.7 million units (*Variety,* 1988c), and MPAA (1988) data put the 1987 sale of pre-recorded videocassettes at 110 million units, up 31% from 1986 (and over 3,500% from 1980!). Although industry analysts see home video growth slowing down, EIA estimates anticipated 1988 cassette sales of 130 million units worth a total of almost $3 billion (*Variety,* 1988c). Figures of this magnitude have a decided effect on movie producer-distributors and can be expected to have an influence on how they handle the release of movies to theaters, as well as to these newer methods of exhibition.

A somewhat similar situation exists with pay-TV and pay-per-view (PPV). Pay-TV is, of course, an economic innovation, not a technological one, but was facilitated by technological developments such as cable television and communication satellites. Upon payment of an optional extra fee, a cable subscriber has access to a package of program services not available on the basic service. PPV is a further refinement whereby a cable subscriber is able, either by using addressable equipment or through telephone ordering, to purchase content on a per-program rather than a per-month basis (as is the case for pay-TV). By the mid-1980s, pay-TV networks reached slightly more than 40 million U.S. homes — or 27.4% of all TV homes according to A.C. Nielsen (Zahradnik, 1987) — while PPV networks reached somewhat over 7 million. Pay-TV has been dominated by such movie-oriented operations as Home Box Office, Showtime/The Movie Channel, Cinemax and the Disney Channel, and PPV firms have an even stronger orientation toward recent theatrical movies. The movie producer-distributors are somewhat schizophrenic about these operations. Several of the majors, for example, invested in the largest PPV network, Request Television, but the studios are generally reluctant to make too great a commitment to this service given its relatively small base and their fear of undercutting home video as a major source of revenue after making major investments in that sector (Frankel, 1986). Once the direction of developments in these areas becomes clearer, however, the potential for greater profit participation than is available for home video (limited by the First Sale Doctrine that precludes their receiving a share of video rental revenues) is likely to have some impact on the movie industry's approach to both videocassettes and theatrical exhibition.

Current and future technological advancements in transmission facilities and home receivers should make consumption of movies in the home even more attractive. Large screen TVs (in both projection and direct-view models) are becoming more prevalent, and size and quality seem to increase each year. TV sound has been improved immensely and stereo has become a widely available feature. Although only 7% of total U.S. sets in 1987 had this feature, estimates put this figure at 30% in 1991 and 40% by the mid-1990s (Polon

Research International estimates cited in Snyder, 1987). Spurred by improvements in VCR picture quality, and moves by some producers to adopt the technology, broadcasters stepped up efforts to identify an appropriate transmission system for high-definition TV (HDTV) in the late 1980s. HDTV offers better picture detail, sharpness, and clarity by increasing the resolution of the television screen image to the 1000 to 1500 scanning line range from the U.S. standard of 525 lines (Stegemen, 1984). Given the costs of development and implementation (not to mention equipment replacement), HDTV is not expected to arrive in the immediate future. As an interim measure, Toshiba and NEC propose to introduce Improved Definition TV (IDTV) in the late 1980s. Employing double-scanning noninterlace technology, IDTV is a kind of half-way step toward HDTV.

ADVANCES IN THEATRICAL MOVIE TECHNOLOGY

A standard attitude expressed by the movie industry, when they were threatened by competition from television, was that theatrical movies could and must offer the potential audience member something that television could not. This attempt at differentiation was found in the realm of subject matter via the "adult" themes that could not find their way onto television screens in the 1950s and early 1960s. This tendency was escalated in the late 1960s and the 1970s, as moviemakers competed with the more prevalent depiction of violence and greater attention to sex in television programs, by increasing both violence and sex and combining them. The dramatic increase in Restricted and X-rated movies is testament to that trend (Edmunds and Strick, 1977). With the growth of the in-home delivery systems (videocassettes and videodiscs), however, the sex and violence market may disappear for theatrical movies.

It was estimated, for example, that in the 1970s up to 60% of movies bought by video recorder owners was of X-rated material (Windsor *Star*, 1979c). This percentage dropped significantly in the mid- to late-1980s as the overall market for videocassettes expanded dramatically. It is estimated that pornographic videos dropped from 25% of the total video market in 1980 to 10% in 1986, but the dollar value of this segment of the industry increased from $50 to $600 million in that period. Moreover, estimates put the weekly U.S. viewership of such materials at 16-20 million people — or 7 or 8% of the entire population. During roughly the same 1980-86 time frame, the number of adult-only theaters shrunk by 67% (Farhi, 1987). It seems that the audience for this content chose to consume it in the privacy of their homes rather than potentially suffer the stigma of attending such movies at a theater. These developments completely undermine Martin's (1977) speculation that explicit sex movies will be one of only two viable theatrical markets in the 1990s, and emphasize the pitfalls of making such futuristic projections on the theatrical movie industry — or any other topic.

A second attempt at differentiating movies from standard television fare involved innovations in the technology of the movie "experience." Competition from television in the early 1950s was met with the introduction of a large number of different formats of wide screen and multiscreen in which the standard screen aspect radio of 1.33:1 (that is, three times high to four times wide) was stretched as far as 2.85:1 in such formats as Cinerama, Super Panavision, Super Technirama, and the like (Limbacher, 1978). By the 1970s, however, this plethora of formats for theatrical movies had been reduced to two: the 2.35:1 aspect ratio using the 35mm Panavision and Todd-AO anamorphic system (originated by Cinemascope) and the 1.85:1 derived by cropping the top and bottom of the standard 35mm frame (DiGiulio, 1976). Until relatively recently, 70mm was the largest movie size used commercially, and due to its compatibility with 35mm, the two had become standard theatrical projection widths in the mid-1950s (Kloepfel, 1976).

The world's largest projection system is now IMAX (for "image maximization"), a 70mm horizontally rather than vertically oriented system. In one of its applications it was used in rear projection to fill a 65-foot by 90-foot screen in the U.S. pavilion at EXPO '74 in Spokane, Washington (Lightman, 1974). Generally the system's image is capable of being projected ten times the size of a conventional 35mm screen, and three times the size of a 70mm one (IMAX Systems Corporation, n.d.); typically the picture is over five stories high and seven stories wide (Lippin Group, 1986). It has made impressive displays at various world fairs and expositions, but permanent installations have been confined to museums, theme parks, and special locations (Lerch, 1986). By the mid-1980s there were 23 IMAX and 22 OMNIMAX theaters in 13 countries. (The latter system is a variation of IMAX, using a 180° fisheye lens to project images onto 86% of the surrounding tilted dome screen similar to that of a planetarium.) Construction plans call for another 25 theaters by the late 1980s, bringing the total world-wide to 70. Seating capacity in IMAX theaters ranges from 120 to 980, with larger ones of up to 1400 seats anticipated; the capacity for OMNIMAX theaters is smaller—in the 94- to 500-seat range, due to their dome structure and the steeply raked seating—although larger facilities are planned (Lippin Group, 1986).

Such large images undoubtedly provide the viewer with a visual experience that cannot be derived from the home screen. There is some evidence to suggest, however, that with these large images the incorrect design of the theater (Szabo, 1976) and the improper location of seating in relation to the screen (Vlahos, 1973) could actually annoy the audience member. Vlahos' research, for example, suggests that a viewer will prefer viewing a movie from a position that is neither too close to the image nor too far away from it to destroy its quality or "information capacity." This distance varies according to the gauge (width) of the movie film, such that "for the 35mm film the preferred viewing positions extended from a near of four picture widths to a far of seven picture widths. On the 70mm film the preferred viewing positions were from two to four picture widths" (Vlahos, 1973). The ironic point here is that "television has conditioned . . . viewer [seating]preferences," since the comparison of movie information capacity is made to the smaller television image (Vlahos, 1973:7). As a consequence, many present theater seats are too close to the screen and more preferred seats could be created farther away.

One final visual innovation which was also introduced in the 1950s, and has been utilized sporadically since, is stereoscopic photography which results in 3-D projection. While promoted by some as a vital possibility in the movie industry (Oboler, 1974; Symmes, 1974), 3-D has always been a recurrent but ultimately short-lived "gimmick." Vlahos (1974) claims this is a result of the fact that the movies' standard storytelling techniques (for example, camera movements, zooms, and changes of shot) are undesirable in 3-D since such techniques do not allow the eyes to focus long enough to derive the maximal effects. In fact, he suggests that 3-D is an entirely different medium from movies, thereby requiring an entirely different "aesthetics." Even the much-touted development of holographic images would not seem to help in this regard — at least in the short to medium term — since a number of technical problems "make the outlook for 3-D holographic movies and TV very bleak" (Holm, 1974:464). Technical improvement of 3-D (such as those seen in the Kodak pavilion at EPCOT) demonstrate that advances can be made in picture quality and the viewing experience; however, the restricted content of these exhibitions and the failure of such mainstream efforts as *Jaws 3-D* and *Spacehunter* suggest that this exhibition format has not been able to transcend its status as a cyclical novelty.

"THE SECOND COMING OF SOUND"

As Schreger (1978) notes, the major obsession in America in the late 1970s was sound, and the movies responded. Catering to a youth market raised on hi-fi and stereo music, the movie industry wished to cash in on the music boom which had amounted to $3.5 billion in 1977 — $1 billion more than U.S. movies for the same period (Schreger, 1978). Although the music industry went through the down portion of its cyclical pattern in the late 1970s and early 1980s, it rebounded somewhat after that with the emergence of the compact disc, and in 1987 earned revenues of $5.57 billion (McLellan, 1988) — well over $1 billion more than the U.S. box office gross for the same period.

Developments had been so numerous and occurred so quickly that it seemed an innovation was no sooner introduced than it was surpassed or supplanted by another: stereo, quadraphonic, quintaphonic, Dolby, Sensurround, Sound 360, Acoustic Sound Recording. The proliferation of various reproduction systems was such that Kolb (1979) listed 24 possibilities encompassing both magnetic and optical sound in 35mm and 70mm formats — four of which were obsolete and four of which at the time had been demonstrated but were not in use.

The most important development in this regard has undoubtedly been the introduction of the Dolby noise-reduction system (Allen, 1975). Dolby has been used for many years in the sound recording industry to reduce "hiss" since "it reduces background noise and improves frequency responses, allowing for sharper highs and lows" (Schreger, 1978:36). First used in rock-oriented movies (such as *The Grateful Dead* and *Tommy*), Dolby was soon more widely adopted by moviemakers who wanted to make use of its increased power, clarity, and subtlety; to create what director Michael Cimino has called "a density of detail of sound" which can "demolish the wall separating the viewer from the film" (Schreger, 1978:36).

The maximal use of Dolby requires that sound be considered from the very beginning of the conceptualization of the movie, right through to its exhibition in the theater. *Star Wars* was the first such movie to really do that (Allen, 1977), and Schreger (1978) refers to it as Dolby's *Jazz Singer*. It was also notable for the degree to which the fact that the Dolby system had been utilized was promoted to attract viewers. (The marquee for *Star Wars* at the Americana theater in metropolitan Detroit, for example, had a yellow flashing "Dolby Stereo" notice. Dolby is the new star, Schreger says.) Such a strategy would seem to have been useful since an informal Twentieth Century-Fox survey indicated that Dolby-equipped theaters significantly outgrossed non-Dolby houses featuring the movie (Schreger, 1978). As Frayne et al. (1976:527) point out, if the Dolby optical stereo system were accepted as the industry projection standard, "theater installations would be less expensive and the soundtrack would remain tamper-proof."

As additional evidence of the growing importance of sound in movies, Schreger notes the example of films being shown in 70mm to take advantage of that format's better sound quality, and the development of Cine-Fi, an improved sound system for drive-ins (that bane of movie enthusiasts), that transmits a movie's soundtrack through the car's radio. And in a post *Star Wars* development, sound recording experts used a 24-track, time-base-code system to record the soundtrack and album of *The Wiz*, "making it possible for the first time to offer the listener true audio stereo images in the exact perspectives as they occur during performance" (Swedien, 1978:1096).

The next major innovation also owed its development to *Star Wars'* creator, George Lucas. THX was a theatrical sound system designed by Lucasfilm's Tomlinson Holman — the acronym standing for Tomlinson Holm cross-over, as well as Lucas' first feature, *THX-1138* (Duncan, 1986). According to Wolf Schneider (1984), "Not since the development of Dolby or the A4 monitor a generation ago has there been such a dramatic improvement in sound playback for movie audiences." The system is treated as a package involving not only the quality of the speakers, but also their placement and suspension, the material in the theater's walls, the makeup of the room itself, and the amount of background noise. Incorporating a new bass cabinet design, adding a component known as a biradial horn, biamping the system and tying it all together with Lucasfilm's crossover network. THX expands Dolby's dynamic range by two octaves with more controlled direction of sound — giving a life-like quality that puts the audience in the midst of the action (Duncan, 1986; Schneider, 1984). All of this is achieved for only the additional cost of 3% when building a new theater. In keeping with Lucas' insistence on high standards, however, movie theaters could not simply apply to purchase the system; they had to qualify by "meet[ing] certain acoustical standards so that Lucasfilm is sure that THX will sound the way it should" (Schneider, 1984).

THE FUTURE MOVIEGOING AUDIENCE

In Chapter 3 it was noted that the movie audience tends to draw its members most heavily from the younger, better-educated, and more economically prosperous segments of the population. This situation is, of course, merely an extension of a trend that was evident as early as the 1940s (Handel, 1950). In attempting to speculate about the size of the future audience for theatrical movies then, it can perhaps be safely assumed that such a trend will continue — although some possible changes are noted below.

Projections of future population demographics are somewhat useful here, although the age breakdowns utilized do not have a perfectly comparable category to the movies' all important 12-29 age grouping. Both Taeuber (1972) and the Organization for Economic Co-operation and Development (OECD) (1975) project that the year 2000 will witness slight declines in the 15-24-year-old category, and slight increases in the 25-44-year-old category (in the case of Taeuber) and in the 25-44-year-old category (in the case of OECD). Brown (1976) cites U.S. Bureau of the Census projections for the 1975-1990 period which foresaw significant changes in only the 30-45 and 65-and-over age categories. The United Nations Department of International Economic and Social Affairs (1982) projects a marginal decline from the mid-1980s figure in the 10-29 age group for the year 2000 and a small increase for the year 2025. Moreover, these changes are not projected to be consistent across subgroups within this age category: the 10-14 and 15-19-year-old age strata will both increase at these benchmark years while the 20-24 and 25-29 subgroups will have lower numbers in the year 2000, but rebound to about their mid-1980s levels in 2025. According to these UN calculations, the 30-and-over age category will have increased markedly beyond its mid-1980s level by both those years (almost 24% by the year 2000 and over 50% by 2025), with only the 40-49 subgroup not exhibiting consistent growth over the 40-year period.

As Taeuber (1972) points out, however, these changes will fluctuate over the intervening decades as a given age group passes through the various age categories (for example, as the members of the 15-24 group move into the 25-44 group as a decade passes). In the case of the 15-24-year-old stratum (the one closest to the MPAA's magic 12-29 age groupings), the decade from 1965-1975 should have witnessed a significant increase in numbers, the decade from 1975-1985 a slight decline, the one from 1985-1995 a slight increase, from 1995-2005 a substantial increase, and from 2005-2015 a marginal increase. Calculations based on the United Nations (1982) data for the 10-29-year age group reveal a similar pattern for these decade-to-decade changes, except for 1985-1995 when a small decrease rather than a slight increase is projected. The prime *potential* audience for movies could be expected to fluctuate accordingly, as could the *actual* audience, *all other things being equal.*

One of these "other things," of course, is education. Those with higher education (particularly those with some college or more) are more frequent movie attenders. Fortunately for the movies, it would appear, the U.S. adult population with some college training increased from 15% of the adult population in 1960 to 25% in 1975, and by 1990 it is expected that "over one-third of the adult population will have had a year or more of college level work" (Brown, 1976:31). U.S. Bureau of the Census (1986:121) figures indicate that the percentage of the population completing one or more years of college actually surpassed one-third of the population in 1985. By that year 35.7% of all persons 25 years old and over had completed at least one year of college, and in the 1975-1985 period the total annual college enrollment of persons 14 years old and over had increased from 10.88 million to 12.52 million — or by slightly over 15%. In the early 1990s, however, enrollment figures were expected to return to the levels of the late 1970s/early 1980s (U.S. Bureau of the Census, 1986:138).

Changes in income distribution have not been as pronounced as those for education, but the direction of the change is somewhat hopeful from the perspective of the moviegoing audience. In the 1975-85 period, the annual median income level of U.S. households (in constant 1985 dollars) fluctuated very little from the 1975 figure of $25,585. During that decade, however, the highest income category ($50,000 and over) was the only one other than the lowest level (under $5,000) to experience an increase rather a decrease in its share of U.S. households, moving from 11.5 to 14.8% (U.S. Bureau of the Census, 1986:431). Such a development would seem to be a positive sign for the movies, given the propensity of the more affluent to be heavier movie attenders.

It was noted above that determinations of the size of the future movie audience were based on the assumption that current trends with regard to the demographics of attendance would hold. Some developments in audience demographics presented in Chapter 3, however, suggest that such patterns may be changing in a manner that bodes well for theatrical movies in the future. The conventional wisdom is that movies are essentially a social experience for the young, and the prime audience is in the 12-29 age group. As Table 3.2 indicates, however, the proportion of total yearly admissions accounted for by individuals age 30 and over had risen from about one-quarter of the total in the 1970s to over one-third by the mid 1980s, with the figure approaching 40% for 1987. It may be the case that the better educated and more affluent young people steeped in the movie culture that began in the 1960s are retaining the moviegoing habit to a much greater extent, even as they assume the heavier responsibilities of family and work that generally accompany increasing age. Hollywood would seem to have recognized this audience trend in that the 1988 summer season witnessed fewer movies than usual aimed at teenagers and more aimed at adults (Harmetz, 1988a). It should be remembered, however, that the youth audience constitutes the vast majority of frequent moviegoers — over 60% in Canada (Newspaper Advertising Bureau, 1986) — and that this approximately 20% frequent moviegoing segment of the total audience accounts for over 80% of the annual admissions.

Nevertheless, if one also looks at the extreme end of the age spectrum, there are some additional heartening signs. A survey of senior citizens (62 years of age and older) in Ontario, Canada indicated that 35% goes to the movies — although the frequency of attendance was not noted and this percentage was much lower than the 80-90% for participation in family- and friend-oriented activities (United Senior Citizens of Ontario, 1985). However, 45% of current moviegoers indicated a desire to increase its involvement in moviegoing (second only to the desire to increase involvement in travel), and 23% of those who didn't currently attend movies indicated a desire to do so.

Other indicators suggest possibilities for the future. On the positive side — in Canada at least — the Gallup poll reported that 38% of the 18-29 age group found 1974 movies "more interesting" than those of five years earlier, while only 7% of those 50 and over agreed (*Take One,* 1974b:7). Another Canadian survey of five major English-speaking markets over a decade later indicated that 55% of the respondents felt the most recent film they had seen was either outstanding (18%) or above average (37%) (Newspaper Advertising Bureau, 1986).

The negative signs seemed more prevalent, however. In line with findings from studies conducted in the 1940s concerning the movies' relative unimportance in comparison with other media (reported in Handel, 1950), a 1974 nationwide survey of 10,000 families assessed movies as being *the worst buy* in the economy among a sample of 40 goods and services. "Less than 6% of those polled considered theatrical films a good buy for the price of admission" (*Take One,* 1974a:7). Similarly, a survey by Peter D. Hart Associates for the Public Broadcasting Service in the late 1970s indicated that movies ranked last behind automobiles, magazines, clothing, popular music, and television in the degree of satisfaction they provided (Brown, 1980). Comparable findings emerge concerning people's affinity for the movies as a general recreational or leisure activity. Only 6% of Canadian respondents said going to the movies was its favorite way of spending time (Newspaper Advertising Bureau, 1986); the same percentage of Americans mentioned movies in response to the question: "What is your favorite way of spending an evening?" (Gallup Report, 1986). (This latter result marked a return to the levels of the 1960s after a jump to 9% in the mid-1970s—both well below the figure of 17% for 1938.) A study of the leisure preferences of British youth revealed that only 9% would most like to "go to cinema/theatre/concerts" as a way of spending its spare time (National Youth Survey, 1983). This figure is similar to the one for younger Americans when an age breakdown of that data is considered (Gallup Report, 1986).

Such findings augur poorly if the situation of movie ticket price increases in Toronto in the late 1970s is representative: between 1959 and 1979, the cost of movie admissions rose 375%, which was relatively high compared with price increases for other cultural and athletic activities in the city (Lancashire, 1979). Data for the United States indicate that the average admission price for motion picture theaters had risen by over 73% between 1970 and 1980 and by perhaps as much as an additional 47% between 1980 and 1987. Despite such increases, however, movie attendance increased from some 921 million in 1970 to almost the 1.2 billion level in the early and mid-1980s. (U.S. Bureau of the Census, 1986:217). Motion Picture Association of America data, as cited in Simon (1987), provided more information about these factors for the period between the mid-1970s and the late 1980s: Average ticket prices demonstrated an inexorable and significant (almost 110%) increase between 1974 and 1987. During the same period, total admissions fluctuated somewhat, but remained fairly close to the 1.1 billion level each year. The total box office gross exhibited greater annual variation, but generally increased over that 14-year period. Such increases in revenues, however, were the result of increased ticket prices rather than a meaningful growth in the theatrical audience.

Given the developments in the area of alternate forms of exhibition or delivery of movies to audiences, the comparative attitudes toward theatrical attendance and these other modes are of considerable concern. In the late 1970s, for example, a Gallup poll reported that 63% of the population was interested in seeing current movies at home, with approximately 35% being "very interested," and some 19% preferring such at-home viewing out of an active dislike for movie theaters (*Take One Filmletter*, 1977). Such a situation should not be that surprising, however, given that an Opinion Research Corporation report to the Motion Picture Association of America as early in TV's history as 1957 found that slightly more people (41%) would have preferred to see a movie on *pay or toll* TV than those (40%) who would have preferred to see it in a movie theater (cited in Austin, 1987). Research in Canada in the 1980s revealed a somewhat different situation in which there was a 56 to 42% preference for theatrical over TV exhibition of movies, with the divergence most notable between frequent movie attenders and virtual nonattenders — and a similar but less drastic division between teenagers and adults (Newspaper Advertising Bureau, 1986). In Great Britain, however, this trend away from theaters and toward TV was also identified: 64% thought "the home was the best place to watch a feature film," while 80% agreed that "if a film is good I don't mind where I watch it" (Docherty, Morrison and Tracey, 1986).

Early Hollywood reaction to these new technologies was rather sanguine in that industry insiders felt that the audiences for these outlets would be substantially different from traditional theatrical moviegoers, with the resultant effect of simply adding to the overall audience for movies through these various markets. Stulberg (1978), for example, cited research that indicated only a 15-20% overlap between the pay-TV viewer and the typical weekend moviegoer, with the resultant effect being projected as the stimulation of pay-TV viewing among moviegoers rather than the reduction of theatrical movie attendance. Such a contention would seem to have been supported by the above-noted Gallup poll since, in approximately 40% of the cases, moviegoers had watched on ("free") TV a movie they had previously seen in the theater (*Take One Filmletter*, 1977).

Even if this phenomenon had seemed promising for the *overall, cumulative* audience of a movie, it was not such a hopeful sign for the *theatrical* segment. By the end of the 1970s, industry observers had noted that the success of blockbuster movies appeared to be the result of the "Want to See Again" factor or repeat audience (Pryor, 1979), in which case pay-TV and the in-home delivery formats could simply be shifting repeat viewership away from the theaters. In fact by the mid-1980s, Austin (1986:103) was speculating that "home video technology may limit the tiered release of the movies by ending the financial feasibility of both rerelease and second-run theatrical markets."

ECONOMIC FACTORS

While the expansion of the movie audience through these ancillary markets might have been good news for the production and distribution segments of the movie industry, it was not very heartening for theatrical exhibitors. Some analysts suggested that, in addition to siphoning off repeat viewings, there was a great deal more overlap of initial patronage between the audiences for the new technologies and for theatrical movies than people such as Stulberg were willing to admit. The *Media Science Newsletter* (1979:2), for example, boldly asserted: "Pay cable and all other new forms of TV *will* tend to compete with the theatres." This prediction would seem to have been confirmed by the mid-1980s when Austin (1986) noted that the initial industry optimism about these two allegedly discrete audiences was misplaced and short-lived; his review of the audience research literature on the subject revealed that the demographic profiles of cable and pay cable subscribers and VCR owners all clearly overlapped that of the frequent moviegoer. Under such a "competition scenario," the effects on theaters would very likely be devastating. The impact of "free" TV on theatrical movie attendance might be somewhat informative here, even if the situations might not have been exactly the same.

In one of the few empirical studies of the impact of TV on moviegoing, Belson (1958) found that the introduction of TV in Britain reduced movie attendance by 33% and reduced interest in attending by 21%. In addition, of the 50 activities Belson examined to determine TV's impact upon them, moviegoing was the most affected and the least able to recover and reestablish its former place in the social life of the population — perhaps as a result of a basic *substitutability* of TV and movie-viewing for a large segment of the population. The consequences of this impact of TV in Britain were aggravated by a kind of "multiplier" effect in which the closures of theaters further contributed to the downward spiral of attendance (Spraos, 1962). This phenomenon is a consequence of the interdependence of supply and demand in the case of the movies, unlike the situation in most other industries. Spraos (1962:128) explains the connection and its consequences in greater detail:

> The volume of admissions depends on the locational convenience and range of choice offered by cinemas in a certain area. Both of these are decreased by a closure. If, as tentatively suggested by the evidence . . . we take it that when 10% of (randomly distributed) cinemas close, there is a loss of 5% in admissions directly attributable to the closures, the spiral chase between contracting capacity and the volume of admissions which it is propelling downwards *can only end when contraction is twice as large as the initial excess capacity* [italics added].

It might be argued that the situation of movie theaters has changed significantly since Spraos examined the British situation, in that theaters are really no longer a neighborhood phenomenon and the general condition of a reduced supply of movies that existed then was not the situation of the late 1980s — although the number of movies produced had been much smaller in the late 1970s and early 1980s (see Figure 2.1), producing cries of a product shortage by exhibitors. It seems to be the case, however (as noted in Chapter 2) that regardless of the total number of movies available in a given year, *relatively few pictures* garner the vast majority of revenues and profits, and are the movies most coveted by exhibitors. In that sense there is a *chronic short supply* of *highly desirable product.* Nevertheless, although the consequences might not be of the same magnitude in the 1980s and beyond as they were in the 1950s, it would be foolhardy for the exhibitors to believe that the principle did not apply to some extent. This is especially important in light of Spraos' (1962:42) suggestions that the British distributors seemed content to let many theaters die to protect themselves in a situation of a shrinking supply of movies — all the more ominous given the producer-distributors' move back into exhibition and the "consolidation" among those firms that was emerging in the late 1980s (both of which trends were discussed in Chapter 2).

Carried to its ultimate extreme, of course, this situation could lead to the complete disappearance of movie theaters. It should be rather obvious that this will not occur. In fact, the 1980s witnessed a boom in theater construction, although Guback (1987a) has noted that total seating capacity still constituted only a bit more than half what it had been in 1948. There is a possibility, however, that theatrical movies will continue to suffer losses to the newer audiovisual media — and may begin to resemble more minority-oriented cultural experiences such as legitimate theater, ballet, and opera.

Austin's (1986:98) extensive review of the impact of the new technologies on moviegoing led him to conclude that a combination of cable, pay cable, VCRs and SMATV (Satellite Master Antenna TV) — a space-age variant of cable — "are and will continue to make, a significant impact on moviegoing. To the film industry what this means is an overall decline in the number of ticket sales and fewer blockbuster movies." This impact would be greater upon less frequent or occasional moviegoers than on frequent ones, whose increased overall leisure time will require them to reduce their moviegoing only moderately while still devoting more leisure time to in-home activities. Moreover, Austin's specific conclusion about the ceiling on the decrease in moviegoing due to cable, and the persistence of a core movie audience can probably be generalized to all these competitive technologies. Figures on U.S. movie attendance for the 1974-87 period are somewhat informative in this regard: for this 14-year span, admissions fell somewhere between the 1 and 1.2 billion marks in all but one year — when they dropped slightly below one billion in 1976 (MPAA data cited in Simon, 1987).

The basic reason for the movies' persistence, in the face of what might be regarded as technological redundancy, is the fact that moviegoing and home viewing are *not* completely substitutable *experiences* or "cultural equivalents." The history of the mass media would indicate that the various forms are complementary rather than completely competitive. While the introduction of a new medium may shrink the audience for and cause alterations in the structure and operation of one or more of the media that preceded it, each medium eventually adapts to the changed environment, reaches its own level, and continues to attract its own specialized audience (for more information on this see DeFleur and Ball-Rokeach, 1987 — although they predict the disappearance of today's movie theater altogether!). Teenagers and young adults will probably always want to escape the confines of the home, and others will more than likely continue to be motivated to seek out an experience which allows intense individual involvement with little risk within an appealing social context.

There is also a more pragmatic factor specific to the movies which would seem to guarantee their continuance. As was demonstrated in some detail in Chapter 2, the major producer-distributors play the primary role in establishing terms and conditions in the seller's market that now exists in the movie industry. These majors seem to have realized that the movies' potential profits can be maximized by capitalizing on the appeal that they generate at the theatrical box office — in Austin's (1986:103) terms, box office performance "is the product value criterion which determines fee schedules for subsequent forms of release." Although some analysts have identified the phenomenon of "video hits" — i.e., movies that did poorly at the box office or received no theatrical distribution at all, but were very successful in the home video market — it does seem to be the case that most movies that are successful in these "ancillary" markets are ones that generated a modicum of success at the theaters.

It is this notion which has caused the majors to plan the play-off or release of a movie *among* the various exhibition media with the same care as they do *within* the theatrical market itself. By the early 1980s, it became standard practice to license movies to the home video market *before* the pay-TV market and only a few months *after* their theatrical release. The assessment had been made that

> the home video market has grown enough in the last year to seriously contend with pay-TV and therefore the timing of home video breaks is now crucial if the consumer is to buy or rent cassettes and discs, something he will not do if he sees it on pay-TV first [*Filmworld,* 1980:4].

The standard four-step pattern (theaters, pay-TV, network TV, syndication) had been replaced by a five-step pattern with home video being inserted between the theaters and pay-TV. It has been noted already that in certain instances release via syndication has pre-empted network TV exposure, and although pay-per-view (PPV) cable had not been a great success nor widely utilized by the late 1980s, experiments had been attempted with simultaneous theatrical release and pay-per-view exhibition. Expectations were that once PPV homes reached an adequate "critical mass," the higher profit participation by the film industry in this market than in home video would induce them to release to this "window" before releasing to videocassettes (Zacks, 1986). The most appealing of Hollywood fare would even get a second exposure on pay-TV after broadcast TV airing or first-run syndication, following which they would go back into syndication (Zacks, 1986).

The emergence and growth of pay-TV and videocassettes in the 1980s had altered the financial base of the motion picture industry. As demonstrated in Table 6.1, the contribution of these two markets to overall motion picture revenues began its climb in the early 1980s, while conversely that of box office rentals declined precipitously, falling below 50% in 1985. (Interestingly, the estimates of Paul Kagan Associates, Inc. for 1984 differ significantly in the figures for box office, pay-TV and home video, putting them at 56%, 19% and 12% respectively. The Kagan figures for 1978, however, are almost identical to the ones in Table 6.1 [cited in Donahue, 1987].) After

Table 6.1 The Market Contributions to Total Revenues for Theatrical Movies

Market	Year							
	1978[a]	1980	1983	1984	1985	1986	1987E	1988E
Box office rentals	80%	76%	57%	51%	43%	40%	42%	43%
Home video	0	1	16	26	34	39	39	38
Pay-TV	2	5	12	11	11	10	8	8
Network and syndicated TV	14	14	9	8	8	7	7	7
Other	4	4	6	4	4	4	4	4

[a]Computed from partial figures supplied by Zacks (1986).
SOURCE: Goldman, Sachs & Company

bottoming out in 1986, box office was expected to increase its contribution to overall revenues slightly while cassettes would level off, then decline a small amount; pay-TV would also decline somewhat despite the potential of pay-per-view, as its true impact would not be known until the early 1990s when the market reached the necessary critical mass (Simon, 1987). In pursuit of profit maximization from its product, the movie industry can be expected to juggle these various windows — and factor in any new ones that emerge — to derive the optimal formula, changing arrangements as conditions vary.

The future of the movies must also be gauged with an understanding of the conglomerates which these majors are, or within which they are embedded. Half of the dozen "organizations" that Monaco (1978:24) selected as "exert[ing the] most control over American media" were (or own companies which were) members of the "majors" which controlled movie production and distribution. These entertainment giants can probably be expected to become involved in many more facets of the leisure and entertainment industry as developments such as videocassettes, videodiscs, and pay-TV advance — and others yet undreamed of are introduced — and pressures toward diversification continue. Madsen (1975) has combined the conglomerate structure of such organizations with the "synergistic" interaction of the various media products (that is, a product in one medium generating a related product in another medium similar to the way that tie-ins have been used to promote movies) to create a vision of the new entertainment industry. He labels this new form "congeneracy" to denote the entertainment industry's evolution into "a communications service providing books, records, movies, radio, television and other sources of electronic information not yet invented or just on the drawing boards" (Madsen, 1975:151). The movies' centrality in the mass media mix (as illustrated in Figure 1.2) would seem to put them at the forefront of such a "service."

The validity of Madsen's contention was given dramatic confirmation in late July, 1989, when a Delaware Court gave final approval for one media conglomerate, Time Inc. to acquire an even larger media giant, Warner Communications Inc. in a $14 billion acquisition. Time will combine its vast holdings in magazines (*Time, Fortune, Sports Illustrated*), book publishing, cable television (including HBO) and broadcasting with Warner's own extensive holdings in motion picture production, distribution and exhibition, the recording industry (including Atlantic Records and the WEA Corporation), and publishing (including DC Comics, the home of Superman and Batman, and *Mad* Magazine). This media giant will control a major portion of the entertainment needs of the American population. It remains to be seen what kinds of interesting synergies or internal conflicts this combination will create. How will *Time* magazine review the films produced by Warner Brothers studios? Will *Mad* magazine be combined with *Fortune*? The next decade should prove to be a volatile one in the entertainment industry.

ALTERNATIVE FUTURES FOR THE MOVIES

Some writers consider the prospects of the movies grimmer than those presented above, agreeing with Spraos (1962:58) that "[t]he cinema, like all things, will die in due course" — *unless* dramatic changes are made in their nature and method of presentation. Holm (1972) is not as radical as many, contending that theaters fairly similar to what we have today will persist, although the development of laser projectors could eliminate the film-based, release print system. Instead, movies could be sent to theaters electronically by cable or microwave — and eventually satellites. In addition, theaters would return to being neighborhood houses in the sense that they would be built in housing and apartment complexes — and would provide babysitting services to attract parents as well as single patrons to the theaters. (This suggestion, however, neglects the consideration that the companies building complexes may be persuaded to choose the installation of pay-TV systems given the probably cheaper costs of installation and more favorable terms that might be offered by pay-TV enterprises.)

Guber (1972:286) also emphasizes the necessity of maximizing the social nature of the moviegoing experience by ensuring that "theatres . . . [are] first-class houses with comfortable seating, and combined restaurants and bars." Such theaters could also become centers for the sale of prerecorded movies (on cassettes and/or discs) since the combination would benefit each. Developments in this direction had occurred to a limited extent by the mid-1980s when, for example, Cineplex-Odeon had started putting "Parisian" cafes into some of its theater complexes — and proudly advertised that they used "real" butter on their popcorn — while a few other theaters sold videocassettes of popular movies over-the-counter, and there was even talk of installing in theater lobbies credit-card activated, automated vending machines that dispensed video movies.

Not only will the exhibitors have to emphasize the social amenities of their theaters, they will also have to rethink the nature of the method of screening so that the patron is "offered a complete show that [is] a totally involving, sensory experience" (Guber, 1972:286). This new method of presentation would be similar to the displays utilizing movies at EXPO '67 in Montreal, EXPO '70 in Osaka, EXPO '74 in Spokane, and at most subsequent world expositions, as well as at popular theme parks such as Disney's EPCOT Center in Florida. Such innovations may require that "the theatre of the future . . . be no more than a hollow shell in which standard elements such as seats and screens are all moveable," and that the road show approach to release be utilized with "giant mixed-media presentations . . . booked in for two years or more and . . . requir[ing] unique interior design" (Guber, 1972:287).

Similar suggestions have emerged from various quarters — all in the vein of differentiating the theatrical movie experience from the home-viewing experience along the technological dimension. *Media Science Newsletter* (1979) presented four strategies to maximize these differences in light of the expected competition from pay cable. One approach would involve the development of multimedia experiences which exploit the "innate excitement of being in a crowd." A second strategy would be the development of interactive devices that would allow viewers to participate in the creation of special effects as they sit in their seats. A third technique would be the combination of movies with live theater and music. Finally, in keeping with the modern narcissistic attitude, audience members waiting to enter the theater could be videotaped by robot cameras and giant-screen video blowups of them could be used at appropriate points as inserts into the presentation.

Many of these techniques have been employed in nonmainstream, experimental situations. The developments at several world expositions have already been alluded to briefly. Many of these involved multimedia presentations utilizing multiple movie and slide projectors, sophisticated stereo sound systems, multiple screens, 360° screens, 360° sound, and so on. One of the EXPO '67 pavilions, Labyrinth, had two huge screens at right angles to one another, with one along the floor and the other standing vertically (*American Cinematographer*, 1967b). Spectators watched and listened in four tiers of balconies along each side of the screens, the highest one being 40 feet above the lower screen. The Carousel Theatre at the same exposition placed the audience "in a merry-go-round turntable which move[d] through six chambers where single and multiple screens present[ed] a filmic panorama of Canada's colorful history" (*American Cinematographer*, 1967a: 552). The Czech pavilion introduced "KinoAutomat," a kind of "decision" theater in which the movie stops at several points and the audience votes as to which of two plot alternatives should be followed, necessitating 78 reels of film to encompass all the possible plot configurations.

A similar theatrical display was attempted at the Trans-Lux Experience Theater in New York in 1974 (*SMPTE Journal*, 1975) and an even more complete movie-sound environment was created in Ecosphere, a "full-sphere" production in which moving images were produced in absolutely *all* directions with the entire room, including the floor, becoming a screen (Carroll, 1974). This "theatre that performs" was created for the Portland General Electric Visitor Information Center of the Trojan nuclear power plant. The theater was actually a quarter of a hemisphere which used mylar mirrors on the floor and the walls to reflect the image which was projected onto the huge, curved, triangular screen. The sound was quadraphonic and a moog synthesizer was employed to assist in the creation of the sound track. It was found, however, that this method of projection suffered from problems similar to 3-D in that transitions had to be slow, cuts used sparingly, and the cameras had to be kept still—to allow the audience to react to changes in the environment.

These movies are a type of "kinaesthetic cinema" which Youngblood (1970:97) defines as "the manner of experiencing a thing through the forces and energies associated with its motion [as presented via the film or video medium]." Such "cinematic experiences" have had little success with audiences in North America, however. The technological limitations on traditional movie storytelling techniques and the general confinement of subject matter to nature and science subjects (perhaps as a result of the former) mean that such systems have high initial novelty value which wears out rather quickly. North American audiences are too accustomed to feature-length, fictional, narrative movies in which attention is *consciously diverted from technique and focused on subject matter.* Such innovations will only be successful in the long term if they can be adequately incorporated into existing storytelling techniques—as 3-D has not (Vlahos, 1974). Alternately, audiences must be socialized into the "new aesthetics" of these multimedia experiences. The prospects of this occurring are not terribly hopeful, however. The ingrained North American (and perhaps even international) bias in favor of a cognitively rather than perceptually oriented notion of "meaning" seems to be catered to most successfully by the narrative form of dramatic fiction.

The future of the movies, then, is basically uncertain, although some very broad possibilities have been outlined. It is important to note that this future will be determined by the conjunction of numerous technological, demographic, and economic factors—the most important of which are within the influence of the most powerful segment of the movie industry, the major producer-distributors. While theatrical movies may not die, they are probably bound to change, perhaps profoundly. All that can be hoped is that the changes which are made do not totally destroy the fundamental pleasure of "one of the few tribal rituals left in America" (Chernow, 1977:33).

REFERENCES

ALLEN, IOAN (1977) "The Dolby sound system for recording *Star Wars*." American Cinematographer 58, 7 (July): 709, 748, 761.

——— (1975) "The production of wide-range, low-distortion optical soundtracks utilizing the Dolby noise reduction system." SMPTE Journal 84, 9 (September): 720-729.

ALLEN, ROBERT C. (1982) "Motion picture exhibition in Manhattan, 1906-1912; beyond the nickelodeon," pp. 12-24 in Gorham Kindem (ed.) The American Movie Industry: The Business of Motion Pictures. Carbondale: The University of Illinois Press.

——— (1980) Vaudeville and Film 1895-1915: A Study in Media Interaction. New York: Arno Press.

American Cinematographer (1967a) "Carousel Theatre." 48, 8 (August): 552.

——— (1967b) "Labyrinth." 48, 8 (August): 548-550.

ANDREW, DUDLEY (1984) Concepts in Film Theory. New York: Oxford University Press.

——— (1976) The Major Film Theories. New York: Oxford University Press.

AUSTIN, BRUCE A. (1989) Immediate Seating: A Look at Movie Audiences. Belmont, CA: Wadsworth.

——— (1987) Pre-publication Manuscript for Immediate Seating. Belmont, CA: Wadsworth.

——— (1986) "The film industry, its audience, and new communication technologies," pp. 80-116 in B. A. Austin (ed.) Current Research in Film. Volume 4. Norwood, NJ: Ablex.

BALDWIN, JAMES (1976) The Devil Finds Work. New York: Dial Press.

BALIO, TINO (1976) "Retrenchment, reappraisal, and reorganization: 1948-," pp. 315-331 in T. Balio (ed.) The American Film Industry. Madison: University of Wisconsin Press.

BARNOUW, ERIK (1968) The Golden Web. New York: Oxford University Press.

BARRETT, MICHELE, PHILIP CORRIGAN, ANNETTE KUHN, and JANET WOLFF (1979) Ideology and Cultural Production. New York: St. Martin's Press.

BARRON, FRANK (1978a) "Worldwide merchandising yields heavily for factors." Hollywood Reporter (April 12): 9.

——— (1978b) "Big movie houses going way of dinosaurs; minis reign." Hollywood Reporter (April 6): 15.

——— (1978c) "Movie-themed films aimed at large record-buying audience." Hollywood Reporter (March 22): 1, 16.

BAXTER, JOHN (1968) Hollywood in the Thirties. New York: A. S. Barnes.

BEAUPRE, LEE (1978) "Industry." Film Comment 14, 5 (September-October): 68, 70, 72, 77.

——— (1977) "How to distribute a film." Film Comment 13, 4 (July-August): 44-50.

BELKIN, LISA (1987) "Ernest goes to the big screen — in a big way." Windsor Star (June 27): F1.

BELLER, MILES (1979) "Cartoon superheros capture Hollywood." Toronto Globe and Mail (December 31): 13.

BELSON, WILLIAM A. (1958) "The effects of television on cinema-going." AV Communication Review 6, 2 (Spring): 131-139.

BERGMAN, ANDREW (1971) We're In The Money. New York: Harper & Row.

BERLYNE, D. E. (1971) Aesthetics and Psychobiology. New York: Appleton-Century-Crofts.

BERNSTEIN, IRVING (1957) Hollywood at the Crossroads. Hollywood: AF of L Film Council.

BERTON, PIERRE (1975) Hollywood's Canada. Toronto: McClelland and Stewart.

BISKIND, PETER (1983) Seeing is Believing: How Hollywood Taught Us to Stop Worrying and Love the Fifties. New York: Pantheon Books.

BLUM, STANFORD (1983) "Merchandising," pp. 378-384 in J. E. Squire (ed.) The Movie Business Book. Englewood Cliffs, NJ: Prentice-Hall.

BLUMER, HERBERT (1951) "Collective behavior," pp. 167-222 in A. M. Lee (ed.) New Outline of the Principles of Sociology. New York: Barnes and Noble.

——— (1935) "Moulding of mass behavior through the motion picture." American Sociological Society Publications 29, 3 (August): 115-127.

——— (1933) Movies and Conduct. New York: Macmillan.

BOGART, LEO (1968) "Mass media in the year 2000," pp. 409-422 in D. M. White and R. Averson (eds.) Sight, Sound, and Society: Motion Pictures and Television in America. Boston: Beacon.

BORDWELL, DAVID, JANET STAIGER, and KRISTIN THOMPSON (1985) The Classical Hollywood Cinema. New York: Columbia University Press.

BOYER, PETER J. (1979) "Buck Rogers in space means money in the bank." Windsor Star (September 20): 14.

BOYLE, BARBARA D. (1983) "Independent distribution: New World Pictures," pp. 285-292 in J. E. Squire (ed.) The Movie Business Book. Englewood Cliffs, NJ: Prentice-Hall.

BRANIGAN, EDWARD (1975) "Formal permutations of the point-of-view shot." Screen 16, 3 (Autumn): 62-68.

BRENNAN, LORIN (1988) "2nd generation video piracy: export assns. move to strike back." Variety (January 20): 159, 160.

BROWN, GEORGE H. (1976) "Demographic pressure for change." Economic Outlook USA 3, 2 (Spring): 30-31.

BROWN, LES (1980) "TV viewers more selective and critical, survey shows." Toronto Globe and Mail (January 3): 13.

BUCK, JERRY (1978) "Free TV plugs help sell movies." Windsor Star (January 4): 15.

BUCKLE, G. F. (1926) The Mind and the Film. London.

BURZYSKI, MICHAEL H. and DEWEY J. BAYER (1977) "The effect of positive and negative prior information on motion picture appreciation." Journal of Social Psychology 101: 215-218.

CALLENBACH, ERNEST (1971) "Recent film writing—a survey." Film Quarterly 24, 3 (Spring): 11-32.

Canadian Motion Picture Distributors Association (1979) A Report on the Distribution of Feature Films in Canada (July).

CARMEN, IRA H. (1966) Movies, Censorship and the Law. Ann Arbor: University of Michigan Press.

CARROLL, STEVE (1974) "Ecosphere: the theatre that performs." American Cinematographer 55, 7 (July): 798-799, 845-847.

CAWELTI, JOHN G. (1976) Adventure, Mystery and Romance. Chicago: University of Chicago Press.

——— (1969) "The concept of formula in the study of popular literature." Journal of Popular Culture 3, 3 (Winter): 381-390.

CERAM, C. W. (1955) Archaeology of the Cinema. New York: Harcourt Brace Jovanovich.

CHADWICK, BRUCE (1983) "Book sells; movie is held." Detroit Free Press (September 12): 2C.

CHERNOW, RON (1977) "The perils of the picture show: fadeout on an era." New York Magazine (August 22): 28-33.

CLARK, CEDRIC (1971) "Race, identification and television violence," pp. 120-184 in G. A. Comstock, E. A. Rubinstein, and J. P. Murray (eds.) Television and Social Behavior. Volume V. Television's Effects: Further Explorations. Washington, DC: U.S. Government Printing Office.

CLARKE, RONALD (1978) "Fotonovel newest gimmick to promote interest in Hollywood movies." St. Catharines Standard (December 27): 34.

COCHRAN, THOMAS C. (1975) "Media as business: a brief history." Journal of Communication 25, 4 (Autumn): 155-165.

COHN, LAWRENCE (1988) "A year of zoom & gloom in pix." Variety (January 20): 1, 92, 94, 99.

— — — (1987) "Pic releases maintain '85 pace." Variety (October 21): 1, 268.

— — — (1985) "Majors up output of in-house pics." Variety (March 20): 3, 26, 27.

COLLINS, RICHARD, JAMES CURRAN, NICHOLAS GARNHAM, PADDY SCANELL, PHILIP SCHLESINGER, and COLIN SPARKS [eds.] (1986) Media, Culture, and Society: A Critical Reader. London: Sage Publications.

COMSTOCK, GEORGE, STEVEN CHAFFEE, NATHAN KATZMAN, MAXWELL McCOMBS, and DONALD ROBERTS (1978) Television and Human Behavior. New York: Columbia University Press.

DALE, EDGAR (1933) Children's Attendance at Motion Pictures. New York: Macmillan.

DALY, DAVID A. (1980) A Comparison of Exhibition and Distribution Patterns in Three Recent Feature Motion Pictures. New York: Arno.

DART, PETER (1976) "The concept of 'identification' in film theory." University Film Association Conference, Iowa State University, Ames, Iowa, August 16-20.

DAVIS, IVOR (1983) "Can $3.2 million buy an Oscar?" Toronto Globe and Mail (April 7): 25.

— — — (1979) "Oscar battle costs dearly." Toronto Globe and Mail (March 24): 35.

De ANTONIO, EMILE (1971) "Some discrete interruptions on film structure and resonance." Film Quarterly 25, 1 (Fall): 10-11.

DeFLEUR, MELVIN and SANDRA BALL-ROKEACH (1987) Theories of Mass Communication. New York: Longman.

DE GRAZIA, EDWARD and ROGER K. NEWMAN (1982) Banned Films: Movies, Censors and the First Amendment. New York: R. R. Bowker.

DEMING, BARBARA (1969) Running Away From Myself. New York: Grossman.

DiGIULIO, EDMUND M. (1976) "Developments in motion-picture camera design and technology—a ten year update. SMPTE Journal 85, 7 (July): 481-487.

DOANNE, MARY ANN, PATRICIA MELLENCAMP, and LINDA WILLIAMS (1984) Re-vision: Essays in Feminist Film Criticism. Frederick, MD: University Publications of America, Inc.

DOCHERTY DAVID, DAVID E. MORRISON, and MICHAEL TRACEY (1986) "The British film industry and the declining audience: demythologizing the technological threat." Journal of Communication 36, 4 (Autumn): 27-39.

DODDS, JOHN C. and MORRIS B. HOLBROOK (1988) "What's an Oscar worth? An empirical estimation of the effects of nominations and awards on movie distribution and revenues," pp. 72-88 in B. A. Austin (ed.) Current Research in Film. Volume 4. Norwood, NJ: Ablex.

DOMINICK, JOSEPH R. (1987) "Film economics and film content: 1964-1983," pp. 136-153 in B. A. Austin (ed.) Current Research in Film. Volume 3. Norwood, NJ: Ablex.

DONAHUE, SUZANNE MARY (1987) American Film Distribution: The Changing Marketplace. Ann Arbor, MI: UMI Research Press.

DRABINSKY, GARTH H. (1976) Motion Pictures and the Arts in Canada: The Business and the Law. Toronto: McGraw-Hill Ryerson.

DUNCAN, ANN (1986) "Theatre sound changes coming." Windsor Star (December 10): B10.

DURWOOD, STANLEY H. and JOEL H. RESNICK (1983) "The theatre chain: American multi-cinema," pp. 327-332 in J. E. Squire (ed.) The Movie Business Book. Englewood Cliffs, NJ: Prentice-Hall.

DYER, RICHARD (1982) Stars. London: BFI Publishing.

EARNEST, OLEN J. (1985) "*Star Wars:* a case study of motion picture marketing," pp. 1-8 in B. A. Austin (ed.) Current Research in Film. Volume 1: Norwood, NJ: Ablex.

EDGERTON, GARY R. (1983) American Film Exhibition and an Analysis of the Motion Picture Industry's Market Structure 1963-1980. New York: Garland.

EDMUNDS, HUGH H. (1979) "Impact and regulation of video-players," pp. 110-121 in J. M. Linton, J. Arvay, D. Baer, and H. H. Edmunds, Jurisdictions and Decision Making in Canadian Broadcasting. Volume 4. Selected Technological, Economic and Regulatory Issues in Canadian Broadcasting/Communications. Windsor, Canada: Centre for Canadian Communication Studies.

— — — and JOHN C. STRICK (1977) "Economic determinants of violence in television and motion pictures and the implications of newer technologies," pp. 71-184 in the Report of the Royal Commission on Violence in the Communications Industry. Volume 7. The Media Industries: From Here to Where? Toronto: Queen's Printer for Ontario.

EISENSTEIN, ELIZABETH (1979) The Printing Press as an Agent of Change. Cambridge: Cambridge University Press.

FADIMAN, WILLIAM (1973) Hollywood Now. London: Thames and Hudson.

FARHI, PAUL (1987) "VCRs bringing porn to homes." Windsor Star (January 17): E8.

FEILITZEN, CECILIA and OLGA LINNÉ (1975) "Identifying with television characters." Journal of Communication 25, 4 (Autumn): 51-55.

FELL, JOHN (1974) Film and the Narrative Tradition. Norman: University of Oklahoma Press.

FELLMAN, NAT D. (1983) "The exhibitor," pp. 313-322 in J. E. Squire (ed.) The Movie Business Book. Englewood Cliffs, NJ: Prentice-Hall.

— — — and STANLEY H. DURWOOD (1972) "The exhibitors: show and teller time," pp. 214-224 in A. W. Bluem and J. E. Squire (eds.) The Movie Business: American Film Industry Practice. New York: Hastings House.

FERKISS, VICTOR C. (1977) Futurology: Promise, Performance, Prospects. Washington Papers V, 50. Beverly Hills, CA: Sage.

Filmworld (1980) "Home video moves up distrib ladder: networks wait longer." (January): 4.

FRANKEL, MARK (1986) "Forcing open a new window." Channels 6, 8 (December): 82.

FRAYNE, JOHN, ARTHUR C. BLANEY, GEORGE R. GROVES, and HARRY F. OLSON (1976) "A short history of motion-picture sound recording in the United States." SMPTE Journal 85, 7 (July): 515-528.

FREDERICKSEN, DONALD L. (1977) The Aesthetic of Isolation in Film Theory: Hugo Munsterberg. New York: Arno Press.

FRIENDLY, DAVID T. (1986) "Crime story's fate a sad chapter in the book-to-movie-market." Toronto Star (August 5): F3.

FURHAMMER, LEIF and FOLKE ISAKSSON (1971) Politics and Film. New York: Praeger.

Gallup Report (1986) Report No. 248 (May).

GANS, HERBERT J. (1974) Popular Culture and High Culture: An Analysis and Evaluation of Taste. New York: Basic Books.

— — — (1957) "The creator-audience relationship in the mass media: an analysis of movie making," pp. 315-324 in B. Rosenberg and D. M. White (eds.) Mass Culture: The Popular Arts in America. New York: Free Press.

GAREY, NORMAN H. (1983) "Elements of feature financing," pp. 95-106 in J. E. Squire (ed.) The Movie Business Book. Englewood Cliffs, NJ: Prentice-Hall.

GERBNER, GEORGE (1967) "An institutional approach to mass communication research," pp. 429-445 in L. Thayer (ed.) Communication: Theory and Research. Springfield, IL: Charles C. Thomas.

GERTNER, RICHARD [ed.] (1987) and (1978) International Motion Picture Almanac. New York: Quigley.

GILES, DENNIS (1977) "The exhibition crisis: the state of the industry." Presented at the Society for Cinema Studies Meeting, Northwestern University, Evanston, Illinois, March.

GOFFA, DEBBIE (1977) "Movie pirates elude the law." Windsor Star (December 21): 16.

GOMERY, DOUGLAS (1986) The Hollywood Studio System. London: Macmillan.

——— (1983) "The American film industry of the 1970's: stasis in the 'New Hollywood'." Wide Angle 5, 4: 52-59.

——— (1979) "The movies become big business: Public theatres and the chain store strategy." Cinema Journal 18, 2 (Spring): 26-40.

GORDON, DAVID (1973) "Why the movie majors are major." Sight and Sound 42, 4 (Autumn): 194-196.

GROVER, RONALD (1988a) "Hitching a ride on Hollywood's hot streak." Business Week (July 11): 44-45.

——— (1988b) "Return of the magnificent seven." Business Week (March 28): 29.

——— (1987) "At Columbia, things might go better with Tri-Star." Business Week (November 30): 74-75.

GUBACK, THOMAS H. (1987a) "The evolution of the motion picture theater business in the 1980s." Journal of Communication 37, 2 (Spring): 60-77.

——— (1987b) "Government financial support to the film industry in the United States," pp. 88-104 in B. A. Austin (ed.) Current Research in Film. Volume 3. Norwood: NJ: Ablex.

——— (1985) "Non-market factors in the international distribution of American films," pp. 111-126 in B. A. Austin (ed.) Current Research in Film. Volume 1. Norwood, NJ: Ablex.

——— (1979) "Theatrical Film," pp. 170-249 in B. M. Compaine (ed.) Who Owns the Media? Concentration of Ownership in the Mass Communication Industry. New York: Harmony Books.

——— (1974) "Film as international business." Journal of Communication 24, 1 (Winter): 90-101.

——— (1969) The International Film Industry. Bloomington: Indiana University Press.

GUBER, PETER (1972) "The cartridge revolution," pp. 25-291 in A. W. Bluem and J. E. Squire (eds.) The Movie Business: American Film Industry Practice. New York: Hastings House.

HAITHMAN, DIANE (1986) "From page to the screen." Detroit Free Press (April 20): 1E, 5E.

HALEY, JAY (1952) "The appeal of the moving picture." Quarterly of Film, Radio and Television 6: 361-374.

HALL, STUART (1982) "The rediscovery of 'ideology': return of the repressed in media studies," pp. 56-90 in Michael Gurevitch, Tony Bennett, James Curran, and Janet Woollacott (eds.) Culture, Society, and the Media. New York: Methuen.

HANDEL, LEO A. (1950) Hollywood Looks at Its Audience. Urbana: University of Illinois Press.

HARMETZ, ALJEAN (1988a) "Hollywood opens its summer onslaught." The New York Times (May 26): C27.

——— (1988b) "Now playing: the new Hollywood." The New York Times (January 10): Section 2: 1, 26.

——— (1987) "Old TV series recycle as movies." Detroit Free Press (March 2): 6D.

——— (1983a) Rolling Breaks and Other Movie Business. New York: Alfred A. Knopf.

——— (1983b) "Invisible marketing helps 'Flashdance' sell." The New York Times (June 4): 15.

——— (1980) "Movie moguls vie for Christmas hits." Windsor Star (November 21): 25.

HARWOOD, JIM (1988) "Hollywood is not Wall Street but money men don't know it." Variety (May 4:) 128.

HASKELL, MOLLY (1973) From Reverence to Rape. New York: Holt, Rinehart & Winston.

HAVELOCK, ERIC (1963) Preface to Plato. Cambridge, MA: Harvard University Press.

HOLDEN, STEPHEN (1987) "Movie music is successful—if it makes people listen." Windsor Star (December 24): B5.

HOLM, WILTON R. (1974) "Holographic motion pictures for theatre and television." American Cinematographer 55, 4 (April): 455, 458-464.

――― (1972) "Management looks at the future," pp. 253-257 in A. W. Bluem and J. E. Squire (eds.) The Movie Business: American Film Industry Practice. New York: Hastings House.

HOLMES, JOHN CLELLON (1965) "15¢ before 6:00 p.m.: the wonderful movies of 'the thirties.' " Harper's (December): 51-55.

HONEYCUTT, KIRK (1979) "Title-testers take over film name game." Toronto Globe and Mail (February 3): 35.

HOUSEMAN, JOHN (1947) "Today's hero: a review." Hollywood Quarterly 2: 161-163.

HOVLAND, CARL I., A. A. LUMSDAINE, and F. D. SHEFFIELD (1965) Experiments in Mass Communication. New York: John Wiley.

HOWE, A. H. (1972) "Bankers and movie-makers," pp. 57-67 in A. W. Bluem and J. E. Squire (eds.) The Movie Business: American Film Industry Practice. New York: Hastings House.

HUETTIG, MAE D. (1944) Economic Control of the Motion Picture Industry. Philadelphia: University of Pennsylvania Press.

HURST, WALTER E. and W. M. STORM HALE (1975) Motion Picture Distribution (Business and/or Racket?!?). Hollywood: Seven Arts Press.

IMAX Systems Corporation (n.d.) IMAX/OMNIMAX Motion Picture Projection Systems. Toronto.

JANUSONIS, MICHAEL (1986) "Music videos sell movies in advance." Windsor Star (August 8): C6.

JARVIE, IAN (1970) Movies and Society. New York: Basic Books.

JOWETT, GARTH (1986) "From entertainment to social force: The discovery of the motion picture, 1918-1945," pp. 1-20 in B. A. Austin (ed.) Current Research in Film. Volume 2. Norwood, NJ: Ablex.

――― (1985) "Giving them what they want: Movie audience research before 1950," pp. 19-36 in B. A. Austin (ed.) Current Research in Film. Volume 1. Norwood, NJ: Ablex.

――― (1982) "They taught it at the movies: Film as models for learned sexual behavior," pp. 209-221 in Sari Thomas (ed.) Film/Culture: Explorations of Cinema in its Social Context. Metchuen, NJ: Scarecrow Press.

――― (1977) "American domination of the motion picture industry: Canada as a test case," pp. 5-13 in S. Feldman and J. Nelson (eds.) Canadian Film Reader. Toronto: Peter Martin Associates.

――― (1976) Film: The Democratic Art. Boston: Little, Brown.

――― (1975) "Toward a history of communications," Journalism History 2, 2 (Summer): 34-37.

――― (1970) "The concept of history in American-produced films: 1950-1961." Journal of Popular Culture 3, 4 (Spring): 799-813.

――― and VICTORIA O'DONNELL (1986) Propaganda and Persuasion. Beverly Hills, CA: Sage.

KAHN, RICHARD (1983) "Motion picture marketing," pp. 263-272 in J. E. Squire (ed.) The Movie Business Book. Englewood Cliffs, NJ: Prentice-Hall.

KAPLAN, E. N. (1983) Women and Film: Both Sides of the Camera. New York: Methuen.

KASUM, ERIC (1983) "There's gold in them thar envelopes: studios heap on the hype, but can an Oscar really be bought?" Detroit Free Press (April 10): 1J, 4J.

KING, RESA and DAVID LIEBERMAN (1988) "Is there more where Dirty Dancing came from?" Business Week (February 15): 110.

KLAPPER, JOSEPH T. (1960) The Effects of Mass Communication. New York: Free Press.

KLOEPFEL, DON V. (1976) "Developments in the design of projection equipment." SMPTE Journal 85, 7 (July): 538-545.

KNOWLTON, CHRISTOPHER (1988) "Lessons from Hollywood hit men." Fortune (August 29): 78-82.

KOEPP, STEPHEN (1988) "Do you believe in magic?" Time (April 25): 66-69, 71-73.

KOLB, FREDERICK J. (1979) "Telecine reproduction of modern picture audio." SMPTE Journal 88, 12 (December): 835-845.

KRIPPENDORFF, KLAUS (1969) "Values, modes and domains of inquiry in communication." Journal of Communication 19, 2 (June): 105-133.

LACHENBRUCH, DAVID (1987) "Sharp and super: a new VCR's got the picture." Channels 7, 11 (December): 124-125.

– – – (1986) "The maker's lament: not-so-fast forward." Channels 6, 8 (December): 88-89.

LANCASHIRE, DAVID (1979) "Costly night at the opera, theatre, ballet, movies . . ." Toronto Globe and Mail (March 24): 31.

LARMETT, JOHN, ELIAS SAVADA, and FREDERIC SCHWARTZ, JR. (1978) Analysis and Conclusions of the Washington Task Force on the Motion Picture Industry. Washington, DC.

LAZARUS, PAUL N. (1983) "Distribution: a disorderly dissertation," pp. 301-309 in J. E. Squire (ed.) The Movie Business Book. Englewood Cliffs, NJ: Prentice-Hall.

LEES, DAVID and STAN BERKOWITZ (1981) The Move Business. New York: Vintage Books.

LERCH, RENATE (1986) "IMAX widens frontier of sensory experience." The Financial Post (February 22): 20.

LEVINE, PAUL G. (1979) "Rock stars rolling into film stardom." Windsor Star (October 6): 25.

LIGHTMAN, HERB A. (1974) "Film at Expo '74." American Cinematographer 55, 10 (October): 1161-1162, 1196-1197.

LIMBACHER, JAMES L. (1978) Four Aspects of the Film. New York: Arno Press.

LINTON, JAMES (1978) "But it's only a movie." Jump Cut 17 (April): 16-19.

– – – (1974) " 'Values . . . theory . . . action! ': Integrating film studies." University Vision 12 (December): 9-26.

– – – and GARTH S. JOWETT (1977) "A content analysis of feature films," pp. 465-580 in the Report of the Royal Commission on Violence in the Communications Industry. Volume 3. Violence in Television, Films and News. Toronto: Queen's Printer for Ontario.

LIPPIN GROUP (1986) IMAX Systems Corporation. New York.

LITMAN, BARRY R. (1979) "The economics of the television market for theatrical movies." Journal of Communication 29, 4 (Autumn): 20-33.

LITWAK, MARK (1986) Reel Power: The Struggle for Influence and Success in the New Hollywood. New York: William Morrow and Company.

LOVELL, ALAN (1970) "The common pursuit of true judgment." Screen 11, 4/5 (July/October): 76-78.

– – – (1969) "Robin Wood – a dissenting view." Screen 10, 2 (March/April): 42-55.

MACCOBY, ELEANOR E. (1968) "The effects of the mass media," pp. 118-123 in O. Larsen (ed.) Violence and the Mass Media. New York: Harper & Row.

MADSEN, AXEL (1975) The New Hollywood: American Movies in the '70s. New York: Thomas Y. Crowell.

MANVELL, ROGER (1971) "The explosion of film studies." Encounter 37, 1 (July): 67-74.

MARTIN, JAMES (1977) Future Developments in Telecommunications. Englewood Cliffs, NJ: Prentice-Hall.

MAY, LARY (1980) Screening Out the Past: The Birth of Mass Culture and the Motion Picture Industry. New York: Oxford University Press.

MAYER, J. P. (1948) British Cinemas and Their Audiences. London: Dennis Dobson Ltd.

MAYER, MICHAEL (1983) "The exhibition license," pp. 338-342 in J. E. Squire (ed.) The Movie Business Book. Englewood Cliffs, NJ: Prentice-Hall.

— — — (1977) "The exhibition license — part II." Take One 5, 6 (January): 29-30.

— — — (1976) "New trends in exhibition deals." Take One 5, 4 (October): 31-33.

— — — (1974) "New trends in exhibition." Take One 4, 5 (September): 48, 50.

— — — (1972) "The exhibition contract — a scrap of paper," pp. 210-213 in A. W. Bluem and J. E. Squire (eds.) The Movie Business: American Film Industry Practice. New York: Hastings House.

MCLELLAN, JOSEPH (1988) "U.S. recording industry is fighting DAT all the way." Calgary Herald (July 28): C2.

McLUHAN, MARSHALL (1966) Understanding Media: The Extensions of Man. Toronto: Signet.

McQUAIL, DENIS (1987) Mass Communication Theory (2nd ed.). London: Sage Publications.

— — — (1984) Mass Communication Theory. London: Sage Publications.

— — — (1969a) Towards a Sociology of Mass Communication. London: Collier-Macmillan.

— — — (1969b) "Uncertainty about the audience and the organization of mass communications," pp. 75-84 in P. Halmos (ed.) The Sociology of Mass Media Communicators. The Sociological Review Monograph 14 (January).

Media Science Newsletter (1979) "How the new TV forms affect moviegoing." I, 3 (May 15-31): 2.

MELLEN, JOAN (1978) Big, Bad Wolves. New York: Pantheon.

MERRITT, RUSSELL (1973) "Nickelodeon theaters: building an audience for the movies." AFI Report (May): 4-8.

MERTON, ROBERT K. (1968) Social Theory and Social Structure. New York: Free Press.

METCALF, STEVE (1988) "Delayed TV shows gives videos a boost." Windsor Star (September 23): C7.

METZ, CHRISTIAN (1975) "The imaginary signifier." Screen 16, 2 (Summer): 14-76.

— — — (1974) Film Language. New York: Oxford University Press.

MONACO, JAMES (1978) "Who owns the media: the conglomerates have a stranglehold on mass entertainment." Take One 6, 12 (October): 24, 26-28, 58-59.

— — — (1977) How To Read a Film. New York: Oxford University Press.

— — — (1974) "Bringing up the baby with the movie camera." Take One 4, 1 (July-August): 32-34.

MORIN, EDGAR (1960) The Stars. New York: Evergreen Press.

MORRISROE, PATRICIA (1980) "Making movies the computer way." Parade (February 3): 16.

MPAA [Motion Picture Association of America] (1988) U.S. Economic Review. New York: MPAA Information Office.

— — — (1987) Incidence of Motion Picture Attendance. New York: MPAA Information Office.

— — — (1979) Audience Study. New York: MPAA Information Office.

— — — (1976) Audience Study. New York: MPAA Information Office.

MULVEY, LAURA (1975) "Visual pleasure and narrative cinema." Screen 16, 3 (Autumn): 14-18.

MUNSTERBERG, HUGO [1916] (1970) The Photoplay: A Psychological Study. New York: Dover Publications.

MURPHY, A. D. (1988) "North American theatrical film rental market shares: 1970-1987." Variety (January 30): 38.

— — — (1983) "Distribution and exhibition: an overview," pp. 243-262 in J. E. Squire (ed.) The Movie Business Book. Englewood Cliffs, NJ: Prentice-Hall.

MYERS, PETER S. (1983) "The studio as distributor," pp. 275-284 in J. E. Squire (ed.) The Movie Business Book. Englewood Cliffs, NJ: Prentice-Hall.

National Council of Public Morals (1917) The Cinema: Its Present Position and Future Possibilities. London: Williams and Norgate.

National Youth Survey (1983) Young People in the 80's: A Survey. London: Her Majesty's Stationery Office.

Newspaper Advertising Bureau (1986) Movie Going in Canada. New York: Author.

NICHOLS, BILL [ed.] (1985) Movies and Methods. Volume 2. Berkeley: University of California Press.

NORTH, C. J. (1926) "Our foreign trade in motion pictures." Annals of the American Academy of Political and Social Science 128 (November): 100-108.

OBOLER, ARCH (1974) "Movies are better than ever—in the next decade." American Cinematographer 55, 4 (April): 453.

O'CONNOR, JOHN (1987) "Program on film-making disguised as documentary." Windsor Star (December 30): C5.

ODDIE, ALAN (1977) "Selling *The Deep.*" Filmmakers Newsletter 10 (May): 26-31.

Opinion Research Corporation (1957) The Public Appraises Movies. New York: Author.

Organization for Economic Co-operation and Development (1975) Demographic Trends 1970-1985 in OECD Member Countries. Washington, DC: Author.

PERKINS, V. F. (1972) Film as Film: Understanding and Judging Movies. Harmondsworth, England: Penguin.

PHILLIPS, JOSEPH D. (1975) "Film conglomerate 'blockbusters.' " Journal of Communication 25, 2 (Spring): 171-182.

POLAN, DANA (1986) Power and Paranoia: History, Narrative, and the American Cinema, 1940-1950. New York: Columbia University Press.

POWDERMAKER, HORTENSE (1950) Hollywood: The Dream Factory. Boston: Little, Brown.

PRICE, MICHAEL H. (1986) "Now the GoBots are in the movies." Windsor Star (March 27): C8.

PRINGLE, D. C. (1979) "Cool millions." TV Guide (December 8): 37, 39-40.

PRYLUCK, CALVIN (1986) "Industrialization of entertainment in the United States," pp. 117-135 in B. A. Austin (ed.) Current Research in Film. Volume 2. Norwood, NJ: Ablex.

PRYOR, THOMAS M. (1979) "Fabulous decade ending in risky multi-million-$ films; Diller on 'Cycles.' " Variety (January 3): 16.

QUIGLEY, MARTIN (1947) "The importance of the entertainment film." Annals of the American Academy of Political and Social Science 254 (November): 65-69.

QUIGLEY, MARTIN JR. (1948) Magic Shadows: The Story of the Origin of Motion Pictures. Washington, DC: Georgetown University Press.

RANDALL, RICHARD S. (1968) Censorship of the Movies. Madison: University of Wisconsin Press.

RATLIFF, RICK (1986) "Which comes first: the toy, the movie or the TV show?" Detroit Free Press (July 14): 5C.

REAL, MICHAEL R. (1977) Mass-Mediated Culture. Englewood Cliffs, NJ: Prentice-Hall.

RORTY, JAMES (1935) "Dream factory." Forum (September): 162-165.

ROSENBAUM, JONATHAN (1980) Moving Places: A Life at the Movies. New York: Harper & Row.

ROSENTHAL, EDMOND M. (1987) "Station competition for movie packages: caution's the word." Television/Radio Age (January 19): 170-173, 434-440.

ROSS, STEVEN J. (1976) "The symposium on movie business and finance." Journal of the University Film Association 28, 1 (Winter): 36-43.

ROSTEN, LEO C. (1941) Hollywood: The Movie Colony, The Movie Makers. New York: Harcourt Brace Jovanovich.

ROTZOLL, KIM B. (1987) "The captive audience: the troubled odyssey of cinema advertising," pp. 72-87 in B. A. Austin (ed.) Current Research in Film. Volume 3. Norwood, NJ: Ablex.

ROWLAND, WILLARD D., JR. (1983) The Politics of TV Violence: Policy Uses of Communication Research. Beverly Hills, CA: Sage Publications.

SAFRAN, DON (1978) " 'Fever' yields merchandising gold; promoter gives input." Hollywood Reporter (July 12): 3.

SAYRE, NORA (1982) Running Time: Films of the Cold War. New York: The Dial Press.

SCHICKEL, RICHARD (1985) Intimate Strangers: The Culture of Celebrity. New York: Doubleday and Company.

SCHILLER, DAN (1977) "Realism, photography and journalistic objectivity in 19th century America." Studies in the Anthropology of Visual Communication 4, 2 (Winter): 86-98.

SCHILLER, HERBERT I. (1976) Communication and Cultural Domination. White Plains, NY: International Arts and Sciences Press.

— — — (1973) The Mind Managers. Boston: Beacon.

— — — (1969) Mass Communication and American Empire. New York: Kelley Publishers.

SCHNEIDER, WOLF (1984) "Sound idea." American Film (December): 9.

SCHREGER, CHARLES (1978) "United Artists' script calls for divorce." Fortune (January 16): 130-133, 136-137.

SCHUYTEN, PETER J. (1978) "United Artists' script calls for divorce." Fortune (January 16): 130-133, 136-137.

SCOTT, JAY (1978) "ERIS can tell a hit — without looking." Toronto Globe and Mail (April 1): 31.

SHAW, TED (1988) "Video doublebill: a beauty and a beast." Windsor Star (October 22): C1, C2.

SIMON, JOHN (1971) Movies Into Film. New York: Dial.

SIMON, RICHARD P. (1988) "Film's financial picture: the fuse has fizzled out." Variety (January 20): 24, 96.

— — — (1987) The Movie Industry — 1988: The End of the Fuse. New York: Goldman Sachs & Co.

SIMONET, THOMAS (1987) "Conglomerates and content: remakes, sequels and series in the new Hollywood," pp. 154-162 in B. A. Austin (ed.) Current Research in Film. Volume 3. Norwood, NJ: Ablex.

— — — (1980) Regression Analysis of Prior Experience of Key Production Personnel as Predictors of Revenues From High Grossing Motion Pictures in American Release. New York: Arno Press.

— — — (1978a) "Performers' marquee values in relation to top-grossing films." Presented at the Society for Cinema Studies Conference, Temple University, Philadelphia, Pennsylvania, March.

— — — (1978b) "Industry." Film Comment 14, 1 (January/February): 72-73.

SISKEL, GENE (1988) "Sneak previews test waters." Houston Post (October 5): 9H.

SMPTE Journal (1975) "The New York experience: a Trans-Lux/Bing Crosby production." 84, 1 (January): 25-27.

SNYDER, ADAM (1987) "Broadcasters are waiting with both ears cocked." Channels 7, 11 (December): 86.

SPRAOS, JOHN (1962) The Decline of the Cinema: An Economist's Report. London: George Allen & Unwin.

STACKHOUSE, FOSTER (1978) "Comics to film to comics." Take One Film-letter 6, 9 (July): 1.

STARK, SUSAN (1983) "Oscar's hype at fever pitch, with $100,000 campaigns." Detroit Free Press (February 4): 3D.

STEGEMAN, ALAN (1984) "The large-screen film: a viable entertainment alternative to high definition television." The Journal of Film and Video 36, 2 (Spring): 21-30.

STEINBERG, COBBETT (1978) Reel Facts: The Movie Book of Records. New York: Vintage.

STERLING, CHRISTOPHER H. and TIMOTHY R. HAIGHT (1978) The Mass Media: Aspen Institute Guide to Communication Industry Trends. New York: Praeger.

STEVENS, JOHN and HAZEL DICKEN GARCIA (1980) Communication History. Beverly Hills, CA: Sage.

STREET, SARAH (1985) "The Hayes office and the defense of the British market in the 1930s." Historical Journal of Film, Radio, and Television 5, 1 (March): 37-55.

STRICK, JOHN (1978) "The economics of the motion picture industry: a survey." Philosophy of the Social Sciences 8, 4 (December): 406-417.

STULBEREG, GORDON (1978) "1980 and beyond—the expanding horizons of theatrical features." American Cinematographer 59, 8 (August): 774-775, 816.

SWANN, PAUL (1987) The Hollywood Feature Film in Post-War Britain. New York: St. Martin's Press.

SWEDIEN, BRUCE F. (1978) "The acoustic sound recording process makes its debut." American Cinematographer 59, 11 (October): 1082-1083, 1096.

SYMMES, DANIEL L. (1974) "3-D: cinema's slowest revolution." American Cinematographer 55, 4 (April): 406-409, 434, 456-457, 478-485.

SZABO, WILL (1976) "Some comments on the design of large-screen motion-picture theaters." SMPTE Journal 85, 3 (March): 159-163.

TAEUBER, IRENE B. (1972) "Growth of the population of the United States in the twentieth century," pp. 17-88 in C. F. Westoff and R. Parke, Jr. (eds.) The Commission on Population Growth and the American Future Research Reports. Volume 1. Demographics and Social Aspects of Population. Washington, DC: U.S. Government Printing Office.

Take One (1974a) "The news page." (March): 7.

——— (1974b) "The news page." (January): 7.

Take One Filmletter (1977) "Two polls." 5, 9 (April/May/June): 3.

Television/Radio Age (1986) "Movie prices level off; barter packages continue to surface." (July 21): 41-43, 77-78, 80.

THOMAS, BOB (1979) "Studios plugging for Oscars." Windsor Star (January 16): 10.

THOMAS, MARK (1987) "Homevid buyers flock to Mifed, find prices steep, competition up." Variety (November 4): 33-34.

THORP, MARGARET (1939) America at the Movies. New Haven, CT: Princeton University Press.

TOEPLITZ, JERZY (1974) Hollywood and After: The Changing Face of American Cinema. London: George Allen & Unwin.

Toronto Globe and Mail (1979) "Radio Star Wars series planned." (April 30): 18.

TRIPP, JENNY (1979) "Hot books: the studios scramble to get first crack at the next block buster." Take One 7, 6 (May): 29-32.

TUDOR, ANDREW (1974a) Image and Influence. London: George Allen & Unwin.

——— (1974b) Theories of Film. London: Secker and Warburg in association with the British Film Institute.

——— (1969) "Film and the measurement of its effects." Screen 10, 4/5 (July/October): 148-149.

TUNSTALL, JEREMY (1977) The Media are American. New York: Columbia University Press.

TYLER, PARKER (1944) The Hollywood Hallucination. New York: Simon & Schuster.

United Nations Department of International Economic and Social Affairs (1982) Demographic Indicators of Countries: Estimates and Projections as Assessed in 1980. New York: Author.

United Senior Citizens of Ontario (1985) Elderly Residents in Ontario: Their Participation in Leisure Activities and the Barriers to Their Participation. Toronto: Minister for Senior Citizens Affairs, Seniors Secretariat.

U.S. Bureau of Census (1986) Statistical Abstract of the United States: 1987. Washington, DC: U.S. Government Printing Office.

U.S. Department of Commerce, Social and Economic Statistics Administration, Bureau of Economic Analysis. Survey of Current Business. Washington, DC: U.S. Government Printing Office.

VARDAC, A. NICHOLAS (1949) Stage to Screen. Cambridge, MA: Harvard University Press.

Variety (1988a) "Major distribs picking up more indie productions but many others never see a screen." (February 24): 66.

Variety (1988b) "VCR penetration up 9% in Canada." (January 27): 34, 36.

Variety (1988c) "Slower growth forecast for homevid business in 1988." (January 13): 33.

VLAHOS, PETRO (1974) "The role of 3-D in motion pictures." American Cinematographer 55, 4 (April): 435, 490-492.

— — — (1973) Psycho-Physical Factors in Photographing and Viewing Motion Pictures. Technical Bulletin No. 11. National Film Board of Canada.

WALKER, ALEXANDER (1970) Stardom. New York: Stein & Day.

WANGER, WALTER (1939) "120,000 American ambassadors." Foreign Affairs 18 (October): 45.

WASKO, JANET (1982) Movies and Money: Financing the American Film Industry. Norwood, NJ: Ablex.

WEIGALL, ARTHUR (1921) "The influence of the kinematograph upon national life." Nineteenth Century (April): 661-672.

WILSON, JOHN M. (1979) "The dollar game." Windsor Star (August 4): 13.

Windsor Star (1988) "Craze for E.T. simmers down . . . temporarily." (November 11): C7.

— — — (1986a) "Oscars may snub big studios again." (December 17): B7.

— — — (1986b) "Comedies flex their muscles." (July 17): C11.

— — — (1986c) "Revue of pop trends enjoyable video fare." (March 20): C15.

— — — (1983) "Paramount backs new drama project." (March 29): B11.

— — — (1979a) "Movies and novelists jump into bed together." (December 3): 11.

— — — (1979b) "The Oscar really is real, real gold." (July 20): 15.

— — — (1979c) "Sex is selling videocassettes." (June 11): 11.

— — — (1979d) "Big toy buyers constantly hunt for hot sellers." (January 24): 46.

WOLFENSTEIN, MARTHA and NATHAN LEITES (1950) Movies: A Psychological Study. New York: Free Press.

WOOD, ROBIN (1969) "Ghostly paradigm and H.C.F.: an answer to Alan Lovell." Screen 10, 3 (May/June): 35-48.

WORTH, SOL (1971) "Film as a non-art: an approach to the study of film," pp. 180-199 in J. S. Katz (ed.) Perspectives on the Study of Film. Boston: Little, Brown.

YARROW, ANDREW L. (1987a) "The studios' move on theaters." The New York Times (December 25): D1, D10.

— — — (1987b) "Chains seek film house dominance." The New York Times (December 17): C19.

YOUNGBLOOD, GENE (1970) Expanded Cinema. New York: E. P. Dutton.

ZACKS, RICHARD (1986) "Picture windows." Channels 6, 2 (May): 40-41.

ZAHRADNIK, RICH (1987) "Great expectations: one more time." Channels 7, 11 (December): 117.

ZIMBERT, RICHARD (1983) "Business affairs and the production/financing/distributing agreement," pp. 175-188 in J. E. Squire (ed.) The Movie Business Book. Englewood Cliffs, NJ: Prentice-Hall.

INDEX

ABOUT THE AUTHORS

GARTH JOWETT is Professor of Radio-TV-Film at the School of Communication, University of Houston, where he was Director from 1980 to 1985. He obtained his Ph.D. in history from the University of Pennsylvania, and has served as Director of Social Research for the Canadian Government Department of Communications. He has published widely in the areas of film, popular culture and propaganda studies. His major work, *Film: The Democratic Art,* first published in 1976 (and republished in 1984), is considered to be the most detailed social history of moviegoing currently available and has become the standard reference work on the subject. He is also the co-author (together with Victoria O'Donnell) of *Propaganda and Persuasion,* a widely used introduction to the subject of propaganda. He has just completed a book on the history of mass culture. In 1987-88, Dr. Jowett received a residential fellowship from the Gannett Center for Media Studies where he completed the research for his new project — a book entitled *Television and America: A Social History of Television.*

JAMES M. LINTON is Associate Professor of Communication Studies, University of Windsor, where he was Department Head from 1981 to 1988. He holds degrees in political science from York University (Toronto) and in communications from the Annenberg School of Communications, University of Pennsylvania. His research and publications have covered a wide range of communication and film areas, including the documentary, communications policy, processes of media production and reception, ethnographic media, cameras in the courtroom, and communication and culture. He has conducted research for a number of government agencies and departments, produced videos for use as evidence in legal proceedings, and been involved in the production of internationally broadcast, award-winning documentary films.